Simon M. Saunders

Domestic Poultry

Being a practical Treatise on the preferable Breeds of Farm-Yard Poultry

Simon M. Saunders

Domestic Poultry
Being a practical Treatise on the preferable Breeds of Farm-Yard Poultry

ISBN/EAN: 9783337140885

Printed in Europe, USA, Canada, Australia, Japan

Cover: Foto ©ninafisch / pixelio.de

More available books at **www.hansebooks.com**

DOMESTIC POULTRY:

BEING

A Practical Treatise

ON THE

PREFERABLE BREEDS OF FARM-YARD POULTRY,

THEIR HISTORY AND LEADING CHARACTERISTICS

WITH

COMPLETE INSTRUCTIONS FOR BREEDING AND FATTEN-ING, AND PREPARING FOR EXHIBITION AT POULTRY SHOWS, ETC., ETC.;

DERIVED FROM THE AUTHOR'S EXPERIENCE AND OBSERVATION

BY

SIMON M. SAUNDERS.

NEW AND ENLARGED EDITION.

———•♦•———

VERY FULLY ILLUSTRATED.

———•♦•———

NEW-YORK:
ORANGE JUDD & CO., 41 PARK ROW.
1867.

Entered according to Act of Congress, in the year 1866, by
ORANGE JUDD,
in the Clerk's Office of the District Court for the Southern District
of New York.

TO

Dr. EBEN WIGHT,

OF BOSTON,

*Corresponding Secretary of the Massachusetts Horticultural Society,
Etc., Etc.,*

THIS LITTLE WORK IS MOST RESPECTFULLY, AND BY PERMISSION,

DEDICATED,

IN RECOGNITION OF HIS SERVICES TO

AMERICAN POULTRY FANCIERS.

GOLDEN RULES.

Never over feed.

*Never allow any **food to** lie about.*

*Never feed from trough, pan, **basin, or** any vessel.*

***Feed only** while the birds will run after the **feed, and not at all if** they seem careless about it.*

Give adult fowls their** liberty **at daybreak.

Never purchase eggs for hatching purposes until a hen is ready to sit.

*For seven or eight days before hatching, sprinkle the eggs **with cold** water while the hen is off. This will prevent the **frequent** complaint **that the chicken** was dead in the shell*

INTRODUCTORY.

The object of the present treatise is, to present a simple description of the various useful breeds of domestic poultry, exhibiting plainly and practically the best methods of their management, and the determining the purity of the variety selected for rearing by the young poultry fancier. Most of the poultry books of the day are voluminous, valuable chiefly to those acquainted with the subject. Their minute accounts of breeds of poultry seldom seen on this continent, tend to swell the pages of the book without the dissemination of practically useful knowledge. In this treatise, I have endeavored to avoid, as much as possible, such a superfluity. Yet I do not place myself before the public as a rival to the numerous writers on the subject. I pretend not to rival them—the field (like the world) is wide enough for all. A few portions of the work must necessarily treat of the same subjects as theirs, although a good deal that is new, I trust, will be found. I have given, with my own experience, that of well known poultry fanciers and "hen-wives," among which will be found that of C. N. Bement, Miss E. Watts, Mrs. Ferguson Blair, John Baily, M. Jacque, and Mariot Didieux. My aim is to furnish a brief but authentic and reliable work on poultry, without embarrassing the reader with useless theories and projects not feasible, and with the hope that my labors may not be found useless, I place my unpretending work before my readers.

S. M. SAUNDERS.

Port Richmond, Staten Island, N. Y.

AUTHORS CITED.

Allen, Hon. L. F., on Dorkings 42
Bailey, John, on Brahmas 35
Bailey, John, on Dorkings 45
Brent, B. P., on Dorkings 42
Columella, on 5-toed Hens 43
Didieux, Mariot, on Dorkings 46
Dixon, E. S., on Dorkings 47
Douglas, John, on Roup and Gapes 33
Fuller, Rev. R. W., on Brahmas 37
Geyelin, G. K., (In Appendix) 107
Giles, John, on Aylesbury Ducks 96
Jaque, Charles 71
Millett-Robinet, Madame, on Brahmas 36
Smith, G. B., on Brahmas 34
Thompson, J. C., on Brahmas 38
White, H. G., on Brahmas 40
Wight, Dr. Eben, on Brahmas 38
Wight, Dr. Eben, on Dorkings 46

CONTENTS.

Dedication	3
Golden Rules	4
Introduction	5
Authors Cited	6
List of Illustrations	8
Origin of our Domestic Fowls	9
Poultry Houses	10
Feeding of Poultry	15
Breeding and Management of Chickens	19
Fattening of Poultry	22
Diseases of Fowls	29
Brahma Pootra Fowls	34
Dorking Fowls	41
Spanish Fowls	49
Game Fowls	54
Malay Fowls	60
Cochin China Fowls	62
Hamburgh Fowls	66
Poland Fowls	68
Bantams	70
Leghorn Fowls	73
French Breeds of Fowls—*Crevecœur, Houdan, La Fleche*	75
The Domestic Turkey	81
The Guinea Fowl	86
The Domestic Goose—*China, Bremen, Toulouse*	89
Feeding and Management of Ducks	93
White Aylesbury Ducks	95
The Musk or Muscovy Duck	97
The Rouen Duck	100
Poultry for Exhibition	102
Appendix—Mr. Geyelin's Visit to the Poultry Yards of France	107—116
Terms and Technicalities	117
Index	119

LIST OF ILLUSTRATIONS.

Brahma Pootra Fowls	(Frontispiece)
Boxes for Nests	12
Fowl House, 6×6 feet, Elevation and Plan	14
Hen Coops	20
Coop for Fattening Fowls	22
White Dorking Cock, Single Combed	42
Foot of Dorking Cock	43
Foot of Dorking Pullet	43
Grey Dorking Cock and Hen, Rose Combed	44
Black Spanish Cock	50
Black Spanish Cock, Head of	51
Black Spanish Hen	52
Black-breasted Red Game Cock	55
Malay Cock	60
Cochin China Cock and Hen	63
Poland Fowls—Silver Spangled and Black	69
Group of Bantam Fowls	72
Group of French Fowls	76
Head of Houdan Cock	77
Crevecœur Cock	78
Combs of Crevecœur Cock	79
Comb of La Fleche	80
Bronze Turkey Gobbler	82
Bronze Hen Turkey	84
Toulouse Geese	89
Bremen or Embden Geese	91
Pair of Rouen Ducks	101
Illustration of Terms	11

DOMESTIC POULTRY;

HOW TO REAR AND FATTEN.

ORIGIN OF OUR DOMESTIC FOWLS.

The common fowl is generally supposed to be of Indian origin, and nothing can be learned respecting their ancestry until within a comparatively recent epoch. Nobody really knows the earliest date of their domesticity. Some suppose it must have been coeval with the keeping of sheep by Abel, which view has a reasonable amount of probability, as the oldest son of Japhet was called Gomer, signifying a cock. Aristotle, 350 years before Christ, speaks of them familiarly as "household words." Among the Greeks and Romans the fowl early figured in the public shows. It was dedicated to Apollo, to Mercury, to Æsculapius, and to Mars, and its courage and watchfulness were well appreciated. The Rhodian fowls and those of Delos, Medea and Persia were celebrated for their superiority in fighting, and for the excellency and delicacy of their flesh. Cock-fighting was a diversion in consonance with the tastes of the Romans, and they were as much devoted to it as are the Malays of the present day, who frequently stake their all upon the issue of a single battle. When the Romans, under Julius Cæsar, invaded Britain, they found the fowl and goose domesticated, but these, as also the hare, were forbidden as food.

They are, in fact, one of man's oldest, and most important acquisitions; passing from generation to generation for thousands of years, and branching out into so many varieties that every breeder will find a peculiarity in some of them to please his fancy. It is only on the most valued varieties I mean to dwell, giving brief and explanatory statements of their origin, their peculiarities of plumage, points and form, and of the tests for purity of blood.

POULTRY HOUSES.

It is only of late years that poultry-houses have been much thought of. In large farmyards, where there are cart-houses, calf-pens, pig-styes, cattle-sheds, shelter under the eaves of barns, and numerous other roosting places, not omitting the trees in the immediate vicinity, I do not think they are required, for fowls will generally do better by choosing for themselves; and it is, beyond a doubt, more healthy for them to be spread about in this manner than to be confined to one place. But a love of order on the one hand, and a dread of thieves, foxes, or skunks on the other, will usually make it desirable to have a proper poultry-house.

The exterior is a matter of taste; but internally, the comfort and well-doing of the poultry must be the only consideration, and the higher the house is, the less likelihood there is of disease or taint. Another advantage of having it lofty is, that the currents of air through the building, being far above the fowls, purify the air without interfering with their comfort. They do not like a draught, and if, while they are perching, an opening is made admitting one, they will be seen to rouse up to alter their position, and at last to seek some other place to avoid it.

The best guide in all these things is nature, and an observer will always find that poultry choose a sheltered spot. They also carefully avoid being exposed to cold winds. The poultry-house should not open to the North or East. The perches should not be more than twenty-four inches from the ground. None are better than fir or sassafras poles, about fourteen inches in circumference, sawn in half in the center. They should be supported on ledges, fastened to each side of the house. This affords every facility for removing them for purposes of cleaning, at the same time that it is very simple. All perches should be on the same level, none higher than the other.

My reason for being thus particular in my description of the perch is, that to mistakes in its construction and position many disorders in the feet of fowls may be attributed. For instance, it has been complained that large fowls became lame, and what we term bumble-footed, more especially when carefully kept in poultry-houses. Now, the reason for it is obvious—their perches are too high. In the morning the cock flies from the perch eight to twelve feet high; the whole weight of his body, added to the impulse of his downward flight, brings him in contact with the ground. Often, from the violence of his fall, small stones are forced through the skin of the balls of the feet. They fester, and if that does not occur, they become so tender that the bird dare no longer perch: he roosts on the ground, and, for want of the necessary exercise, his legs swell at the knees, and he becomes a sleepy, useless fowl. This will be avoided by having low perches. Some well-informed authorities deem high perches of no consequence, provided the fowls have a plank with cross-pieces reaching them from the ground. But I believe these are only used to ascend; the descent is generally done by flight.

It is very necessary the house should be well ventilated; it may be done either by an iron grating or an omission of bricks in the building, but the ventilators should be considerably above the perches, and in severe weather may be entirely closed. It is an improvement to have a ceiling to the house; a very slight and common one will do, and it is not absolutely necessary. The house should be often cleaned out, and the walls whitewashed. The floor should be of earth, well rammed down and covered with loose gravel two inches deep. This is easily kept clean by drawing a broom lightly over it every morning, and if it is raked, it is kept even and fresh. There should be an opening towards the West or South for the fowls to go in and out; and this should never be closed, as fowls are fond of rambling early in the morning, and picking up such food as is to be found at break of day.

It should not be allowed that any poultry roost in the house but fowl—no ducks, turkeys, geese, or any other sort. Neither may there be too many fowls, lest the house become tainted and the birds sickly.

The poultry-house should have three compartments; one, the largest, for roosting, another for laying, and another for sitting; though, if it is desired to curtail the accommodations, two compartments might suffice—that is, one for roosting and laying, and the other for hatching—taking care, however, that the nests for laying are not in too close proximity to the roosting-poles. In both the laying and sitting rooms, boxes (as in fig. 1) should be placed against the side of the house, on the floor; all that is required is to fasten up boards against the wall, each being twenty inches high, the same length, and eighteen inches apart. This affords the hen all the privacy she requires. About eighteen inches from the wall a wooden head should be put, just high enough to prevent the eggs from rolling out.

Fig. 1.—BOXES.

It may not be out of place to mention, that, as no hen should be allowed to lay where the others are sitting—and difficulty may be experienced with some, from their almost unconquerable repugnance to sit anywhere but where they have been laying. It may be stopped in this way: move the hen and her eggs at night into the sitting-house, and cover her until morning, by hanging sacks, or old carpets, or matting over the boards forming her sitting-place, and she will remain quiet and satisfied.

The door of the sitting-house should always be shut when hens are on their eggs, and it should, therefore, have a window, to open in the summer, but to shut quite close in the winter. When the window is, however, open, a wire frame or piece of lattice-work, should supply its place, to prevent laying hens from intruding.

There is one addition to a poultry-yard so advantageous to chickens that those who have once tried it will never be without it. I mean a covered run for them, to be used in wet weather. Any sort of roof will do, and it should be in a sheltered spot, running the length of the yard, and projecting six to twelve feet from the wall or close fence against which it is placed. It should be exposed to the sun, and sheltered from cold winds. The floor should be raised above the level of the yard, and covered with sand and wood ashes, some inches deep. The hens with chickens may be put here under their coops, in wet or stormy weather, and it affords at all times a favorite resort for poultry to bask and take their dust-bath, which is essential to their well-doing. The flooring should be higher at the back than the front.

There is nothing better for the bottom of a nest than a sod of grass. On this should be placed straw. A nest so made is healthier for the hen and chickens, as it admits of sufficient ventilation, and is always free from vermin.

It is essential both doors and windows of roosting-places should be open during the day for the purpose of ventilation. The floor should slant every way towards the door, to facilitate the cleaning, and to avoid anything like wet. It should be well cleaned every day, and it should be raised above the level of the surrounding ground; it should have no artificial floor, such as boards, bricks, tiles, or stones of any kind, but should be of good hard earth and loose gravel—not disposed to be muddy from its occupants going in and out in wet weather. It should open on ground perfectly free for the poultry to run in; and if a high dry spot on light soil can be chosen, so much the better. The roof should be quite air and water tight.

Fig. 2.—FOWL HOUSE, 6 × 6.
a, Door; *b*, Ventilators; *c*, Brackets; *d*, Entrance.

It is not necessary to build expensive houses. I keep a cock and five hens in a wooden house. (See fig. 2.) It is seven feet high in the centre, six feet square inside, and is planned as in fig. 3. Such a house will cost, being made of pine wood, about fifteen dollars, and will last many years. It is portable, by passing poles through the brackets, (c, c, Fig. 2) on each side. It has no floor. A coating of tar or paint will prevent the boards from splitting.

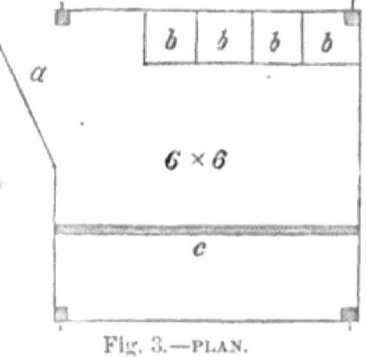

Fig. 3.—PLAN.
a, Door; *b*, Laying Boxes; *c*, Perch.

FEEDING OF POULTRY.

It is difficult to assign any portion of food as a sufficient quantity for a given number of fowls, because so much depends on the nature of their run, and the quantity and quality of food to be found. For instance: in a farmyard where the barn-door is always open, and operations scattering grain and hay seed continually going on, adult birds require little or no feeding; but if the supply be stopped, then they must be fed by hand.

A good healthy growing fowl will consume, weekly, two-thirds of a gallon of corn or wheat; and if the bird come from a yard where it has been but poorly fed, it will, for a time, eat more than this; but after it has got up in flesh and condition, it gradually eats less, and two-thirds, or even half the quantity, will keep it in good condition. Again: the weather must be considered; in mild, damp weather they prowl about and pick up many things—as insects, worms, young herbage. These all assist; but in frosty—and, above all, in snowy weather—they require generous feeding.

Do not spare good food for chickens; they require plenty while they are growing, and they will make a good return in health and **vigor**, when arriving at maturity. Those who are obliged to keep **fowls** in confinement, should have large sods of grass cut, and let the earth be heavy enough to enable them to tear off the grass, without being obliged to drag the sod about with them. Where there is a family, and consequent consumption, there are many auxiliaries, such as bread crumbs, groats that have been used for gruel, etc. But it must be borne in mind, that these are in the place of other food, and not in addition to it. When they can be had, other food should be diminished. I am not an advocate for cooked vegetables, except potatoes. Boiled cabbage is worse than nothing. In fact, it must be borne in mind, corn, either whole or cracked, is the staple food, and the others are helps. Do not give fowls meat; but always have the bones thrown out to them after dinner; they enjoy picking them, and perform the operation perfectly. Do not feed on raw meat. It makes fowls quarrelsome, and gives them a propensity to pick each other—especially in moulting time, if the accustomed meat be withheld. Hundreds have purchased birds—above all, Cochin Chinas—on account of their great weight, which, being the result of meat-feeding, has proved a real disease, incapacitating them for breeding. When proper food is provided, all is not accomplished; it must be properly given. No plan is so extravagant, or so injurious, as to throw down heaps once or twice a day. They should have it scattered as far and wide as possible, that the birds may be long and healthily employed in finding it, and may not accomplish in a few minutes that which should occupy them for hours. For this reason, every sort of feeder or hopper is bad. It is the nature of fowls to take a grain at a time, and to pick grass and dirt with it, which assist digestion; but if, contrary to this, they are enabled to eat corn by mouthfuls, their crops are soon overfilled, and they seek relief in excessive draughts of water. Nothing is more injurious than this; and the inactivity that attends the discomfort caused by it, lays the foundation of many disorders. While speaking of food, it may be observed, that when, from traveling or other cause, a fowl has fasted a long time, say thirty or forty-eight hours, it should not have any hard food, neither should it have water at discretion. For the first three hours it should only have a small portion—say a teacupful of sopped bread, very wet; so much so, as to serve for food and drink. If the bird appear to suffer much from the journey, instead of bread and water, give bread and ale.

But the food given them by hand is not all that is essential. There is the natural food, sought out and divided by the hen to her progeny—such as insects of all kinds, peculiar herbage, etc. And it is here well to remark, that where fowls are bred for exhibition or other special purposes—as cocks for fighting—a hen should not be allowed to rear more than six chickens, as she can not find this food for a greater number; and if they are intended to be superior to all others, they must have greater, or at least equal advantages with those they will have to compete against.

In most poultry-yards more than half the food is wasted. The same quantity is thrown down day after day, without reference to the time of year, alteration of numbers, or variation of appetite; and that which is not eaten, is trodden about, or taken by small birds. Many a poultry-yard is coated with corn and meal. As it is essential fowls should have fresh-mixed food, a careful poultry-feeder will always rather mix twice, than have any left; and it is often beneficial for the birds to have a scanty meal. They can find numerous things wherewith to eke out, and things that are beneficial to them; but if they are kept constantly full, they will not seek them. The advantage of scattering the food is, that all then get their share; while if it is thrown only on a small space, the master-birds get the greater part, while the others wait around.

Many have been discouraged, and some deterred from keeping fowls, by the expense of feeding. If they will themselves attend to the consumption for a week, and follow the method I have pointed out, they may arrive at a fair average; and they will be surprised to find how much greater the cost has been than was necessary. It is most essential not to invent or to supply imaginary wants in fowls. They do not require coaxing to eat; and wherever food can be seen lying on the ground in the yard, there is waste and mismanagement. The economy is not in the food alone. They are large gainers in health, and the pleasure of keeping is much increased. The tendency of over-feeding is to make them squat about under sheds and cart-houses; and instead of spreading over a meadow or stubble in little active parties, searching hedges and banks, and basking on their sides in the dust, with opened feathers and one wing raised to get all the glorious sun's heat they can—they stand about, a listless, pampered group. To lay much better, to breed better chickens, and to last longer, are the results of diminished, not increased expense in feeding; and all that is required is a little personal superintendence at first, till the new system is understood and appreciated. In most yards the birds are overfed, and there is waste in nearly all.

It is common with those who undertake to write upon poultry to be asked: What is the food to make fowls lay? High feeding of any sort will do it, but particularly with hemp seed, scrap-cake, liver, or any meat chopped fine. The scrap-cake, after chopping, should be put in a bucket, and covered with boiling water. The mouth of the bucket should be covered with a double sack, or other cloth, so completely, as to exclude air, and confine the steam till the greaves are thoroughly softened. When they are nearly cold they may be given. These will make them lay, but it is only for a time; premature decrepitude comes on, and disease in many forms appears. The most common is dropsy, and of an incurable character. The fowl that would have laid for years, in the common course of nature, being forced to produce in two that which should have been the work of several, loses all beauty and usefulness; and yet it is often considered matter of wonder that the most prolific hen in the yard should suddenly become barren.

BREEDING AND MANAGEMENT OF CHICKENS.

However reluctant those concerned with poultry may be to acknowledge the fact, it is not the less true that most old women who live in cottages know better how to rear chickens than any other persons; they are more successful, and it may be traced to the fact that they keep but few fowls, that these fowls are allowed to run freely in the house, to roll in the ashes, to approach the fire, and to pick up any crumbs or eatable morsels they find on the ground, and are nursed with the greatest care and indulgence.

The first consideration is the breeding-stock, and I would advise, in an ordinary farm-yard, to begin with twelve hens and two cocks; the latter should agree well together.

Too much pains cannot be taken in selecting the breeding-fowls; the presence of all the characteristics of the various breeds, as described in the following chapters, should be insisted on in the purchasing of stock.

Having the stock, the next point will be breeding. I am a great advocate for choosing young birds for this purpose, and with that view would advise that perfect early pullets be selected every year for stock the following season, and put with two-year-old cocks: for instance, pullets hatched in May attain their growth and become perfect in shape, size and health before the chills of winter. They should be put with cocks of two years old, when they will lay on the first appearance of mild weather, and their produce has the same advantage as these have had before them. I do not advocate having young stock-fowl so much on account of their laying early, as I do for the superiority of their breeding. Neither is it desirable to breed from fowls of all the same age. If it can be done, it is better to put a two-year-old cock with pullets, and *vice versa*.

It is well to introduce fresh cocks of pure breed into the yard every second year; this prevents degeneracy, and for the same reason no cock should be kept more than three seasons, nor hen more than four, if it is intended to keep them in the highest possible perfection and efficiency.

Of hatching I will say but very little, as the hen will do that naturally, and consequently well. An ordinary sized hen will cover thirteen eggs. All nests should be on the ground. Eggs for hatching should not be purchased till a hen is ready to sit. For seven or eight days before hatching, the eggs should be sprinkled with cold water while the hen is off. This will prevent the frequent complaint that the chicken was dead in the shell.

I give, herewith, (Fig. 4,) a sketch of the best coop I have yet found for hen and chickens. Its dimensions should be twenty-four inches high in front, eighteen wide in front, and twenty-four in depth. It should be close everywhere but in the front. That should be made of bars, and the three centre ones should lift up by means of cross pieces.

Fig. 4.—HEN COOP.

It must not have a bottom. The hen should be kept in the coop, or rather under it, at least six weeks, and in the winter the longer she is under the better. The coops should be often moved, as it prevents the ground from becoming tainted.

It is too often presumed that little care is required as to the feeding of poultry from the time they leave the coop until the time they are put up for fattening. They are allowed the run of the yard, without considering what a precarious subsistence this affords. There may be abundance of food at some periods, and little or none at others. They should be fed regularly, and care should be taken that each of them (for they are all brought up either for the table or stock) shall have a fair share.

For chickens, I would recommend for the first week after hatching, a hard-boiled egg to be given, chopped fine at least twice a day, wheat steeped in milk, and coarse Indian meal, bread-crumbs, canary and millet seed, etc., etc. A change of food is not only advantageous, but necessary, and I would advise that twice per week the food be changed, substituting cracked corn for wheat. They must also have constant opportunities of picking among grass and other herbs. They should only be fed so long as they will run after their food; as soon as they are careless about it, they have enough. Fowls in confinement will pine to death with heaps of corn around them, unless they have these opportunities.

As the chickens get older they will require feeding less often, but they must never be allowed to fall off in condition, and after from ten or twelve weeks in the summer, or from fourteen to eighteen in the winter, they will be ready to fatten, if required.

Next, as to water. It is too much the idea that any description will do, and that provided there be some within their reach, though it have been standing a week, nothing more is required. This is a mistake. Water for fowls and chickens should be very clean; the vessel containing it should be well rinsed out every morning; it is a good plan to put a little gravel at the bottom, and it should be changed twice a day. I am aware, many will be disposed to think this unnecessary; but I will ask any one who has the opportunity to try whether, where there is a stream of water running through a yard, they can cause the poultry to forsake it by placing water nearer to their haunts; it will always be found they prefer going to the stream, to drinking out of the pan or tub.

There is little doubt many of the diseases of poultry arise from the filthy water they are often obliged to drink from ponds full of decayed vegetable matter, and tainted by the fall of leaves in autumn from overhanging trees

FATTENING OF POULTRY.

There are two methods of fattening; one is by feeding in troughs, another by cramming. When merely a good useful fowl is required, the first process will suffice; but, when it is wished to make a fowl of extraordinary fatness, such a coop or pen as I shall endeavor to describe will be required. It is represented in the accompanying sketch.

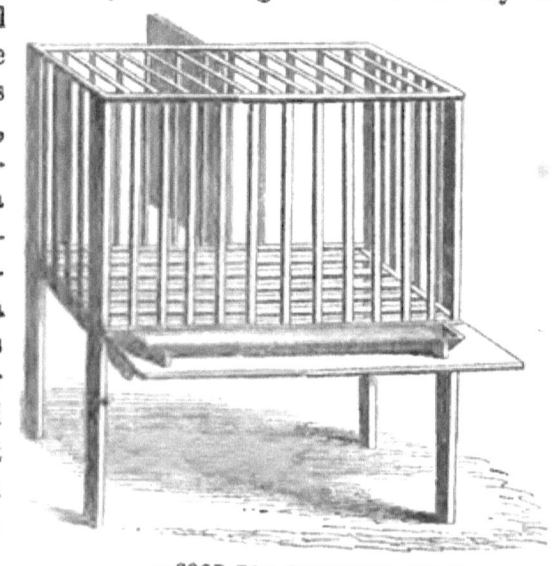

—COOP FOR FATTENING FOWLS.

A coop for twelve fowls should be twenty-four inches high, three feet long, and twenty-two inches deep; it should stand about two feet from the ground, the front made of bars about three inches apart, the bottom also made of bars about an inch and a half apart, to insure cleanliness, and made to run the length of the coop, so that the fowl constantly stands, when feeding or resting, in the positition of perching. The sides, back and top, indeed the whole of the coop should be made of bars, as in the sketch. The bars of which it is made should be an inch and a half wide. Some people make them round, and I am not sure they are not preferable to flat ones. Fattening fowls do not require much room. Exercise is not favorable to the process, and it is, therefore, important that the room given to each bird should be only so much as will enable it to stand up or sit in tolerable comfort. For this reason there are two slides to the coop. These not only make the task of catching the fowls much easier, but they are very useful when the coop is wanted for a smaller number of birds. If only four are required, and they have the same space allowed to them as to twelve, they will make little progress. It is therefore necessary to have a board or division made, which, by passing between the bars from front to back, will make a coop of the size required. There should be a trough made in front of the coop, and I much prefer it wedge-shaped to the square ones generally in use. It is much easier to clean. The coop only requires in addition a flat board running along in front, having a groove cut in it to receive the bottom of the trough, and an upright piece at the edge to support it. The trough must be easily movable, which is necessary, as it must be scalded once every day to keep it sweet.

This trough must be filled three times a day with food, the quantity being regulated by the number of fowls fattening; the food should be coarse meal, mixed slack, but not quite liquid, the consistence being such that if some of it were placed on the flat board in front of the coop, although it would spread, it would not run off. It may be mixed with water, but milk is much better; in fact, it should always be borne in mind the food cannot be too good or too clean. It is also essentially necessary that sound discretion be used in the quantity of food given. No more should be given than is eaten up clean at a time, and at every meal it should be fresh-mixed food. When the time arrives for the mid-day feed, if there remains any uneaten in the trough from the morning, it is proof either that too much was given before, or that the fowls are sick. If the first, let them fast till evening; if the second, alter the character of the food, by mixing it either slacker or stiffer; but in both cases the food which has been left must be taken away, or it will turn sour, and the fowls will take a distaste for it, which will prevent their fattening. There should be pans continually before them containing fresh, clean water; and when the troughs are removed for scalding, and while they are drying, there should be gravel spread on the ledge before them; they will pick out the small stones to assist digestion, which greatly promotes their health.

Another excellent thing is to cut a lot of grass and place it occasionally before them. No better proof will be required of this being good for them, than the avidity with which it will be eaten. All these things assist health, and for a fowl to be good on the table, it must be healthy when alive. By this process, a fowl put up in good flesh and condition will be fat enough for ordinary purposes in about ten or fourteen days.

It will be observed, I inculcate the greatest cleanliness throughout. Cleanliness is one essential; another, that the fowls be fed early in the morning, as soon as the sun rises, for they will be then waiting for their food. If the first meal of a fowl is deferred till seven or eight o'clock on a summer's day, the bird has been hungry, restless, and dissatisfied four hours, and in that time the progress made in fattening the previous day has been fretted away. This remark applies both to picking and the succeeding method of fattening.

The next process is cramming. The coop must be precisely similar to that used for pickers, with troughs. The number of these coops must depend on the supply of fowls that is required, as they should not always be in use, lest they become tainted. They are so inexpensive and easily made, it is not worth while to incur any risk of this sort; and after one has been in use for a month, it is always well that it should be washed, exposed to the air for as long time as it can be spared, and if lime-whited (white-washed), so much the better.

The fowls for cramming are put in this coop, and if wanted very fat in a short time, the best of those fed by the former process may be selected, and in a week they will be very good; but if not in a hurry, then good fleshy young fowls should be put up, and fed as follows: but (in this and the former method) care must be taken to put up fowls that have been accustomed to be together. If strange fowls are put in the same coop they will fight, and if so, they will not fatten; nor is that all, from the continual excitement they will become hard. It will sometimes happen that even a pullet is quarrelsome; if so, she must be taken from the coop and kept separate, or she will interfere with the well-doing of the lot. If fowls are to thrive, they must be warm. The heat and steam of the birds should be perceptible to the hand when it is put in. For this purpose they must be close to each other, and the coop should be covered up with old sacks, carpet, matting, or anything of that sort.

The food is the same as before, viz., coarse meal mixed with milk, the only difference being, it is mixed stiffer, and it must now retain the form given to it; if it is wished to make the fowls very fat, a little mutton-suet may be boiled in the milk with which the meal is slaked. A " cram" should be about the size of a woman's finger, and an inch and a half long. Six or eight are given morning and evening; that is enough to fill the fowl's crop. The crams should be rolled up as dry as possible, and in order to make the swallowing easy, previous to being given they should be dipped in milk. Women perform this operation better than men: the fowl is placed in the lap, the head is held up, and the beak kept open with the thumb and finger, the cram is introduced into the gullet, the beak is then closed, and the cram is gently assisted down till it reaches the crop; care must be taken not to pinch the throat, as ulceration would follow, and the fowl would be spoiled. If at mid-day the fowls appear restless and dissatisfied, a very little food may be given to them in the same way as to those fed by troughs. They must also be well supplied with water and gravel.

It will sometimes happen that when the time arrives for the evening meal, that of the morning has not digested. Therefore, before the second feed is given, the crop should be lightly felt to see if it be empty; if it is not, there is evidence of something wrong. The fowl must be taken out immediately, and the beak being held open as if for cramming, some warm water or gruel should be poured down the throat, and the beak closed. The bird will swallow it, and it will soften the food; but if more food were forced into the crop on that already hardening there, the fowl would become "crop-bound"; that is, the food would become solid and indigestible, and the fowl would be totally spoiled for the table, if it did not die. By the foregoing process, a fowl may be made perfectly fat and good in fourteen to sixteen days. There is no necessity to feed longer, unless large size be desired, when feeding may be continued three weeks. I prefer the former period, because the fowl then is fat enough and in perfect health;

but frequently afterwards, although it will get fatter and apparently larger, it will lose both weight and flesh. The latter becomes red and dry; the internal fat impedes the exercise of the functions of digestion; and the fowl becomes diseased. This is what poulterers call "clung," and arises from disease of the liver, caused by excessive feed There is no possible method by which a fowl may be kept fatting and in perfect health after it has reached the acme of fatness. It must then be killed, or it will become worthless. When put up either for trough-feeding or cramming, the birds must be in some sort of building, and completely sheltered from cold and draughts. When the weather is chilly, they should be covered with sacks or matting, as warmth is very essential in causing them to thrive. Attention to these explicit details will remedy one of the complaints urged against country poultry, viz., that it is too lean.

Another objection urged is, that the flesh is hard. For this complaint there are two causes; first, the poultry is too old; next, it is eaten too fresh. Fowls should be put up to fatten at from twelve to fourteen weeks old in the summer, and from sixteen to twenty in the winter. The difference is caused by the fact that in warm weather they arrive at maturity much sooner than in cold; and when a fowl has arrived at maturity it is too old for the table. It is a mistake to keep a fowl until it is too old for the sake of having it large. It is true it looks handsome on the table, but it is useless there. Perhaps part of the breast may be eaten, but the legs are far too hard to furnish any delicate food. Still, size is much to be desired, and it can be attained by following the rule laid down for feeding chickens well from the first, and the increase in size and weight during the fortnight's systematic fattening is almost incredible to those who have never observed it. But to be tender, the fowl must be young. There is no process by which an old one can be made good for the table, and **surely, though it may be a little** smaller, it is better **to have a good juicy** fowl, which **all will** eat with relish, than **a** larger **one, which,** from its hardness, **cannot** be enjoyed.

Another complaint often **made is that,** although a good **fowl is to be** had sometimes, **there is no** certainty. This arises from the fact that the fowls **are** improperly selected; **that if six** fowls are wanted, they **will** perhaps **be taken from six different broods.** This is very wrong; **the oldest brood should be cleared off before** the next is taken. **It may** be said **there is only a difference of three weeks or a month between them; but in summer and** autumn a month **turns the** pullet **into a hen, and so unfits her for the** table.

The next cause **for their being hard is, they are eaten too** fresh. **I use the term** *fresh* **in a qualified sense. A really young fowl does not** require **keeping to become tender, because it is naturally so;** but, **if eaten the day it is** killed, it **must be stringy, as every member of the** body **is still rigid. Forty-eight hours will be quite long** enough **to keep such a fowl. But in spite of all care, there** will sometimes be fowls beyond **the age I have** specified, as the proper time for killing; and then, by **keeping** them some days, they will become more tender.

An other very important point. **If a fowl be** caught up **out of a** farm-yard, or taken out of coop, **full of food, and killed directly, as is too** much the custom, the food **in the body and crop ferments, and at last corrupts the flesh; but if the bird be fasted—that is, kept entirely without** food or water from **twelve to fifteen hours before it is** killed—it will be found quite empty, and, in moderate weather, will keep from four to six days, during which **period it** becomes tender. In the winter it may kept **much** longer.

DISEASES OF FOWLS.

Among the disease of fowls, nothing is so fatal to the bird, or so vexatious to the fancier, as the Roup. Very close observation and experience have taught me the first premonitory symptom is a peculiar breathing. The fowl appears in perfect health for the time, but it will be seen that the skin hanging from the lower beak, and to which the wattle is attached, is inflated and emptied at every breath—such a bird should always be removed.

The disease may be caused, first, by cold damp weather and easterly winds, when fowls of weakly habit and bad constitution will often sicken, but healthy, strong birds will not. Again, if by any accidental cause they are long without food and water, and then have an unlimited quantity of drink and whole corn given to them, they gorge themselves, and ill health is the consequence; but confinement is the chief cause, and above all being shut up in tainted coops. Nothing is so difficult as to keep fowls healthy in confinement in large cities; two days will often suffice to change the bright, bold cock into the spiritless, drooping, roupy fowl, carrying contagion wherever he goes.

But all roup does not come from cities; often in the spring of the year the cocks fight, and it is necessary to take one away; search is made for something to put him in, and a rabbit-hutch or open basket is found, wherein he is confined, and often irregularly supplied with food, till pity for his altered condition causes him to be let out; but he has become roupy, and the whole yard suffers. I dwell at length on this, because of all disorders it is the worst, and because, although a cure may seem to be effected, yet at moulting, or any time when out of condition, the fowl will be more or less affected with it again. One thing is here deserving of notice. The result of the attention paid to poultry of late years has been to improve the health and constitution of the birds. Roup is not nearly so common as it was, nor is it so difficult of cure. It went on unnoticed formerly, till it had become chronic, and it would not be difficult to name yards that have now a good reputation, but which, a few years since, never had a healthy fowl. It is now treated at the outset, if seen, but the improved management in most places renders it of rare occurence. The cold which precedes it may often be cured by feeding twice a day with stale crusts of bread soaked in strong ale, there must be provided, warm dry housing, cleanliness, nutritive and somewhat stimulating food and medicine. In my own case I generally give as medicine some tincture of iron in the water pans and some stimulants. The suspected fowl should be removed directly, and if there be plenty without it, and if it be not of any breed that makes its preservation a matter of moment, it should be killed. There is very little doubt of a cure if taken in the first stage. But, if the eyelids be swollen, the nostrils closed, the breathing difficult, and the discharge fœtid and continual, it will be a long time before the bird is well. In this stage it may be termed the consumption of fowls, and with them, as in human beings, most cases are beyond cure. However I may differ from some eminent and talented amateurs, I do not hesitate to say it is contagious in a high degree. Where fowls are wasting without any apparent disorder, a teaspoonful of cod-liver oil per day will often be found a most efficacious remedy.

I will next mention a disease common to chickens at an early age—I mean the gapes. These are caused by numerous small worms in the throat. The best way I know of getting rid of them, is to take a hen's tail-feather, strip it to within an inch of the end, put it down the chicken's windpipe, twist it sharply round several times, and draw it quickly out: the worms will be found entangled in the feathers. When this is not effectual in removing them, if the tip of the feather be dipped in turpentine, it will kill them, but it must be put down the windpipe, not the gullet. I have always thought these are got from impure water, and I have been informed by a gentleman who inquires closely into those things, that having placed some of the worms taken from the throat of a chicken, and some from the bottom of a water-butt, where rain-water had stood a long time, under a microscope, he found them identical. I have never met with gapes where fowls had a running stream to drink at. Camphor is perhaps the best cure for gapes, and if some is constantly kept in the water they drink, they take it readily. This has been *most successful*. There is also another description of gapes, arising probably from internal fever; I have found meal mixed with milk and salts a good remedy. They are sometimes caused by a hard substance at the tip of the tongue; in this case, remove it sharply with the thumb-nail, and let it bleed freely. A gentleman mentioned this to me who had met with it in an old French writing on poultry.

Sometimes a fowl will droop suddenly, after being in perfect health; if caught directly, it will be found it has eaten something that has hardened in the crop; pour plenty of warm water down the throat, and loosen the food till it is soft, then give a tablespoonful of castor-oil, or about as much jalap as will lie on a ten cent piece, mixed in butter; make a pill of it and slide it into the crop; the fowl will be well in the morning.

Cayenne pepper or chalk, or both mixed with meal, are convenient and good remedies for scouring.

When fowls are restless, dissatisfied, and continually scratching, it is often caused by lice; these can be got rid of by supplying their houses or haunts with plenty of ashes, especially wood ashes, in which they may dust themselves, and the dust-bath is rendered more effectual by adding some sulphur to the dust. It must be borne in mind, all birds must have the bath; some use water, some dust; but both from the same instinctive knowledge of its necessity. Where a shallow stream of water runs across a gravel road, it will be found full of small birds washing; where a bank is dry, and well exposed to the sun, birds of all kinds will be found burying themselves in the dust.

Sometimes fowls appear cramped, they have difficulty in standing upright, and rest on their knees; in large young birds, especially cocks, this is merely the effect of weakness from fast growth, and the difficulty their long weak legs have in carrying their bodies. But if it lasts after they are getting age, then it must be seen to. If their roosting-place has a wooden, stone, or brick floor, this is probably the cause; if this is not so, stimulating food, such as I have described for other diseases, must be given.

Fowls, like human beings, are subject to atmospherical influence; and if healthy fowls seem suddenly attacked with illness that cannot be explained, a copious meal of bread steeped in ale will often prove a speedy and effectual remedy. For adults, nothing will restore strength sooner than eggs boiled hard, and chopped fine. If these remedies are not successful, then the constitution is at fault, and good healthy cocks must be sought to replace those whose progeny is faulty.

"Prevention is better than cure." The cause of many diseases is to be found in enfeebled and bad constitutions; and these are the consequences of in-and-in breeding. The introduction of fresh blood is absolutely necessary every second year, and even every year is better. Many fanciers who breed for feather fear to do so lest false colors should appear, but they should recollect that one of the first symptoms of degeneracy is a foul feather; for instance, the Sebright bantam loses lacing, and becomes patched, the Spanish fowls throw white feathers, and pigeons practise numberless freaks. An experiment was once tried which will illustrate this. A pair of black pigeons was put in a large loft, and allowed to breed without any introduction of fresh blood. They were well and carefully fed. At the end of two years an account of them was taken. They had greatly multiplied, but only one third of the number were black, and the others had become spotted with white, then patched, and then quite white; while the latter had not only lost the characteristics of the breed from which they descended, but were weak and deformed in every possible way. The introduction of fresh blood prevents all this; and the breeder for prizes, or whoever wishes to have the best of the sort he keeps, should never let a fowl escape him if it possesses the qualities he seeks. Such are not always to be had when wanted, and the best strains we have, of every sort, have been got up by this plan. There is one thing worthy of remark: none of our fowls imported from warmer climates are subject to roup, as Spanish, Cochins, Brahmas, and Malays. But those from a damp country, like Holland, seem to have seeds of it always in them.

The following tonic is highly recommended by Mr. John Douglas of the Wolseley Aviaries, England, to prevent roup and gapes in chickens and old fowls:—"One pound of sulphate of iron, one ounce of sulphuric acid dissolved in a jug with hot water, then let it stand twenty-four hours, and add one gallon of spring water; when fit for use, one teaspoonful to a pint of water given every other day to chickens and once a week to old fowls, will make roup and gapes entirely a stranger to your yards.'"— This may be true if perfect cleanliness is maintained and the fowls are in other respects well treated.

DESIRABLE BREEDS.

BRAHMA-POOTRA FOWLS.
(SEE FRONTISPIECE.)

The origin of the Brahma fowls has been a subject of much contradiction, but has been assigned to the banks of the Brahma-putra, a river that discharges its waters into the Bay of Bengal.

Their first appearance was in the city of New York, in the year 1850, when three pairs were in the possession of a sailor, who sold them to a mechanic in that city, who again sold them or their progeny. By some writers it has been contended that they are nothing but gray Shanghais; this can only be attributed to a desire on the part of the Shanghai and Cochin breeders to put a stop to the rapid advance to favor made by the Brahmas. But it is useless, for they have everything to recommend them, and their lovers and admirers must be content with the good qualities which by universal consent are awarded to them, and though they appeared at a time when people were suffering from the effect of the decline of the Cochin mania, they held their own, and have succeeded in forming numerous and attractive classes. The Brahma is a large, heavy bird, symmetrical, prolific, and hardy; living where Shanghais would starve, growing in frost and snow when hatched in winter months. In speaking of various breeds of fowl, Mr. G. B. Smith says: "As regards Brahmas and gray Shanghai fowl, I think there is a great difference between the two. I have raised them for several years, and greatly prefer the Brahmas. They lay a third larger egg than the Shanghai, and are the best fowl for any one desiring eggs in the winter. Their eggs sometimes weigh from three to four and a quarter ounces each, whereas those of the Shanghai seldom reach over two or two and a half ounces. The Brahmas, I think, will lay a greater weight of eggs in a year than any other fowls I am acquainted with. I have bred fowls for over twenty years, and there are none I like better than these."

That the Brahmas are a distinct breed I have not the least doubt, but whether they come from China or India I will not stop to discuss. It is enough that they come from the East—from Asia.

The deficiency of tail is the characteristic of all these fowls, Cochins, Brahmas, Malays. Even the Jungle fowl (the hyæna for wildness of all Gallinaceæ, and one that can well be called untamable,) although the most favored of his country in the way of tail, carries it drooping. That the eggs are alike in color cannot weigh, because all our Asiatic birds lay cream or chocolate colored eggs. If feathered legs are to prove their identity with Cochins, then from that I would deduce proof of their distinctness. Out of large numbers I have bred, I have never had a clean-legged chicken. Mr. John Baily, purveyor to the Queen of England, says: "I have imported and bred these fowls for two years; I have watched them narrowly, and find they differ in many points from the Cochin, with which they are sought to be identified. They wander from home, and they will get their own living; *they never throw a clean-legged chicken*; they have deep breasts; they lay larger eggs, and they are hardier. I have hatched them in snow, and have reared them out of doors without any other shelter than a piece of mat or carpet thrown over the coop at night.

"From any birds that I have kept, I have never had an untrue chicken, all being more or less gray. They are hatched almost black or yellow, and the dark get lighter and the light darker. I have never had a clean-legged chicken from them."

This breed is much esteemed in England, as also in France, where it was introduced in the year 1853. Madame **Millett Robinet**, authoress of Basse-Cour, writes in the following flattering terms of the Brahmas: "The cock is full of pluck and pride; he is still more developed than the Cochin China; his feathers are also richer and more brilliant. The Brahma Pootra cock, which obtained the first prize at the Universal Exhibition in Paris, in 1856, weighed $10\frac{1}{2}$ pounds, and was sold for 2,500 francs ($500). Brahmas are good layers, good mothers, flesh very abundant, and of a good quality."

Mariot Didieux, in writing of Brahma Pootras, says: "This race came from India about the year 1850, but, as with all beautiful races, speculation has taken hold of them. A couple of the pure race we know was sold at the enormous price of seventeen hundred francs, (equivalent to $340)."

The Brahma Pootra is divided into two varieties, the dark and light; pea, and single combed; the selection of color must be entirely a matter of taste. The cocks of the dark variety have a black breast speckled with white; thighs black; hackle * and saddle † light; tail black and spreading at the end; yellow legs, very well feathered; deep breast, very full hackle. The hens of this variety have bodies pencilled all over; silver hackle—that is, pencilled like the silver pheasant—deep body: yellow legs, well feathered; pea or single combed. The cocks and hens of the light variety are much alike in plumage, but

---

* HACKLE—The feathers growing from the neck and covering the shoulders and part of the back.

† SADDLE FEATHERS—Those feathers growing from the end of the back and falling over the side.

the cock frequently less marked than the hen; entirely white plumage, save the tail, and flight* feathers, which should be black, and the hackle, which should be black striped. These should also have well-feathered yellow legs, and either pea or single combed; the under feathers of these birds should be dark.

The Brahmas are the only fowls that are pea-combed. The pea-comb has the appearance of three combs pressed closely together, that in the centre being higher than the others. Another thing worthy of remark is, that in many of the single combs, close observation will show on either side the plain impression of another, the evident remains of that which had been a pea-comb, and by in-breeding had disappeared.

The Brahma Pootras eat much less than the Cochins, and are amongst the best winter-layers we have; they rank among the very prolific producers of eggs throughout the year; they seem to be as hardy as it is possible for fowls to be, are good sitters and mothers, and good for the table.

The Rev. R. W. Fuller, of Massachusetts, says in a letter to W. N. Andrews, Esq., of New Hampshire: "I have a pair of Brahma Pootra fowls, and I consider them decidedly the most splendid and beautiful fowls ever imported. Their color is white, inclining on the back to a rich cream color, the hackles on the neck slightly streaked with black. The legs are yellow, heavily feathered with white, and shorter than the Chittagong or Shanghai, giving the fowls a more beautiful proportion. They are very gentle and peaceable in their disposition, and have a stately and graceful gait. Take them altogether, they are just the fowls for an amateur to fall in love with, and such as an owner with one spark of vanity would desire to keep in the front yard, that all passers-by might behold and admire them."

---

* FLIGHT FEATHERS—The last five feathers of the wing.

An English writer says: "So much has been said about the Brahma fowl, and such a variety of opinions given as to whether they are a distinct breed or not, that I will venture to say a little respecting them. That they are a distinct breed there is not the least doubt, for long before they were imported into this country, a brother of mine, who has been much in India, informed me of them, and pointed out most particularly the advantages they possessed over the Cochins. I have now several of these birds in my possession, both the dark and the light variety. Some months since my brother visited me, and on being shown the birds, at once pronounced them to be the same as those he had seen in India."

Dr. Eben Wight, of Boston, in a letter speaking of the Brahma Pootra fowls, remarks: "A man in Connecticut says he has a pair, the same stock as Hatches, which he has weighed: cock thirteen pounds; hen nine pounds six ounces; but he refuses to sell them. That is a fine breed of fowls and must beat all others."

Mr. J. C. Thomson, of Staten Island, in writing on Brahmas, says: "As the Brahmas had the reputation of being very hardy and good winter-layers, I determined to try them. In fact, the person in Massachusetts who furnished me with the trio, said he had a hen, in February, hatching a brood in a cold wood-house, when the thermometer was six below zero. So, to try it fairly, I put the old trio in an ash-house, on the shady side of the dwelling, so open that daylight could be seen through all the joints of the boards on the north side, with the upper part of the west side open lattice work. It was the coldest building I had, as no sun shone on it through the winter. A small yard on the west side of the house gave them an opportunity to occasionally bask in the sun, on the lee side of a board fence. Ample food and drink, with a little cabbage, was daily given—grain always within their reach. One laid right on through the coldest weather, the eggs frequently freezing in the nest. The other was evidently a very old bird, from the fact that she moulted in midwinter.

"The ten pullets had better quarters, and grew finely; in March they began to lay, and laid steadily all through the summer. My stock consisted of the three old birds, one spring pullet, and ten September-hatched pullets. Finding they were giving me an unusual number of eggs, especially in June, when I frequently got eight, nine, ten, and eleven, and sometimes twelve eggs a day, I was induced to keep an account for July and August, when I find they have averaged six eggs per day—equal to 2,000 eggs per year. This month I have allowed six of them to sit, the last brood hatching to-day. The experience of last autumn satisfies me that they can be grown with success in the autumn and winter months, as I am able to give them the entire range of the garden; they coming in as early layers in the spring, to take the place of early-sitting hens. The weight of the cocks runs from ten to twelve pounds, and pullets from seven to nine pounds. My year-old (this September) pullets weigh seven and a half pounds, and will, no doubt, during the coming winter run up to eight or nine pounds.

"They are not large eaters, considering their size; after repeated trials, when closed in a small yard, without grass, I find the fourteen head would only eat three pints of grain per day, or a fraction over a bushel each per year, and with a good range a bushel of grain per head would be an ample supply.

"Their very quiet habits are greatly in their favor. A four-foot wire, picket, or lath fence, they seldom get over. If they should, then shorten the feathers on one wing, and there is no more trouble.

"As mothers, they are excellent sitters and nurses—rather heavy when hatching. Chicks should be removed almost as fast as they are hatched, and kept warm till all are out. When with their chicks, they move about as carefully and gracefully as a turkey-hen. Being large and full-fledged, they will, in warm weather, care well for two dozen chicks—in the cooler seasons a dozen will be ample.

"They are more disposed to sit than many other kinds. By shutting them up a few days, giving plenty of food and water, they soon give up and go to laying again.

"As a market-bird, their fine size and plumpness make very desirable table-birds—their flesh, in my estimation, being quiet equal to the very best: in fact, when we take into consideration their winter-laying qualities, with all their other good qualities, they are just the birds for the million. Being fully feathered, even to their toes, protects them against the vicissitudes of our ever-changing climate.

"As a lawn-bird, none excel them in beauty. A flock, viewed from a short distance, gracefully moving about, or quietly sitting in groups, are frequently mistaken for a flock of lambs.

"For crossing, or bringing up the ordinary stock of the country to full fifty or seventy-five per cent. in value, my advice to poultry-growers is, to procure good male birds, remove all others."

Mr. H. G. White, in the Albany *Country Gentleman*, of August 4, 1864, says: "After several years' experience I find this variety well adapted to the general purposes for which fowls are kept.

"They possess size, beauty and hardiness in a great degree, and are very prolific. Their eggs, which are large, surpass all others in richness; and, like most fowls with light plumage and yellow legs, their flesh is of good quality. I have obtained from fifty-five fowls, in the month of March, ninety-two and a half dozen of eggs. They excel all others as winter-layers. I have raised the present season a hundred and twenty-five chickens with quite ordinary care."

To form a just opinion of these fowl, it is necessary to study their habits and to breed them. Enough is seen in their shape to justify us in holding them distinct from the Cochin, but still more do we find it in their habits and produce. As a useful and hardy fowl it is unsurpassed. They are excellent layers of good-sized eggs, good foragers, when they can have their liberty, and good sitters and mothers. The chickens fledge more kindly than the Cochins, grow fast and are exceedingly hardy; old and young take good care of themselves, and by fasting, when abstinence is beneficial, often recover from ailments which would carry off any of a less hardy sort—in fact, I know no other chickens which are so hardy as they, and reared with so little trouble and loss, and I have no hesitation in pronouncing them the most useful fowls for the American farm-yard.

THE DORKING FOWLS.

This breed of fowl was described by Pliny, by Columella, and by Aldrovandus; and has long been known to naturalists as the *Gallus pentadactylus*, or five-toed fowl. The breed is of great antiquity; possibly the "couple of short-legged hens" which Justice Shallow, of Gloucestershire, ordered for the entertainment of Sir John Falstaff, may have at least been closely related to it. Some suppose it to have been introduced by the Romans, as they esteemed a breed of fowls characterized by five toes; and a five-toed variety existed in ancient Greece, for such is noticed by Aristotle.

The name Dorking originated from a town of that name in Sussex, England; but why, cannot be readily answered, for when Camden wrote his Brittania, in 1610, Dorking was so inconsiderable as not even to be mentioned by him, and in his map of Surrey it is marked a mere village. The fame of Dorking poultry was established in England about 125 years ago; and from that time the greatest care and attention have been paid to their breeding.

The first Dorkings brought into the United States were introduced in about the year 1840, by Hon. L. F. Allen, of Black Rock, New York.

WHITE DORKING COCK.

Of the Dorkings there are three varieties; the white, gray, and speckled. The white has been supposed to be *the* Dorking of old fanciers. B. P. Brent says: "The old Dorking, the pure Dorking, the only Dorking, is the white Dorking;" and that the speckled or gray Dorking is a recent and improved cross, by which the size was much increased, between the original white breed and the

Malay, or some other large fowls; but I cannot assent to such a proposition. Columella's favorite sort of hen could not differ much from the speckled Dorkings as they at present exist. He says: "Let them be of a reddish or dark plumage, and with black wings. Let the breeding hens, therefore, be of a choice color, a robust body, square built, full-breasted, with large heads, with upright and bright red combs; those are believed to be the best breed which have five toes."

FOOT OF DORKING COCK.

Columella had the white sort, but he rejected them, for he advises: "Let the white ones be avoided, for they are generally both tender and less vivacious, and also are not found to be prolific;" and such seems to be the prevailing opinion of many poultry-fanciers in the nineteenth century. The gray and speckled Dorkings above referred to have of late been prodigious favorites at all the poultry shows in England and Scotland; and are bred to great size and beauty; in fact, they are larger and heavier birds than the white. When exhibited, rose and single-combed fowls compete together, but it is imperative that all their combs in one pen shall be alike. In plumage, also, the birds in a pen should match, although almost any variety as to color is tolerat-

FOOT OF PULLET.

ROSE-COMBED GRAY DORKING COCK AND HEN.

ed. The gray Dorking is a large, plump, compact, square-made fowl, with short legs and ample furnishing. The fifth toe must be well developed, and quite distinct pointing upwards and not a mere branch of the fourth.— The accompanying illustrations will more lucidly explain the development of the fifth toe. The following is from the pen of Mr. John Bailey, considered the best judge of these fowls in the world: "One of the most popular colors for hens in the present day is that known as Lord Hill's. The body of these birds is of a light slate color, the quill of each feather being white; the hackle is that known as silver, being black and white striped; the breast is slightly tinged with salmon color. The next class is a larger one—the grays. These may be of any color, provided they are not brown; ash cobweb with dark hackle; semi-white with dark spots; light gray, penciled with darker shades of the same color. With all these the most desirable match for a cock is one with light hackle and saddle, dark breast and tail; I advisedly say dark in preference to black, because I think servile adherence to any given color too often necessitated the sacrifice of more valuable qualities. I look on a fine Dorking cock with no less admiration if his breast be speckled and his tail composed of a mixture of black and white feathers; and such a bird is a fit and proper mate for any gray hens—but the gray must not be confounded with the speckle; these have a brown ground with white spots. One of the best judges I know of a Dorking fowl, properly describes them as brown hens covered with flakes of snow. These speckled hens are of two distinct colors, the first is known as Sir John Cathcart's color; the pullets are of a rich chocolate, splashed or spotted with white; the cocks are either black-breasted reds without mixture, or spotted like the hens on the breast and partially on the body; it is no objection if the tail is partially colored—

another speckle is of a grayish-brown spotted with white; these hens should have a cock with dark hackle and saddle, and the wings and back should show some red or chestnut feathers. These last are not essential, but a *light cock* will not match *speckled hens*. Next we have brown hens; these should have a black-breasted red cock, but a speckled one will pass muster."

In the silver gray, the cock should have black breast and tail, and white hackle on neck and saddle. The hen should have a white hackle streaked with black, light gray body, with light shafts to the feathers and a robin breast.

In size, the Dorking ranks next to the large Asiatic tribe. It is short-legged and large bodied, and readily accumulates flesh, which is of a very good quality. Mowbray, when he wrote, ranked them in size in the third degree of the largest of fowls. The weight of the Dorking at maturity varies from five to eight pounds, and full grown Capons have been known to weigh from ten to twelve.

The Dorking hen is rarely a layer of more than twenty eggs, when she becomes broody. The eggs are usually of a clear white, but sometimes of an ashy-gray color, rather larger in size, weighing from $2\frac{3}{4}$ to 3 ounces each; rounded at both ends and of a rich flavor. They are excellent sitters and good mothers. Mariot Didieux, in his "Practical Guide for the Rearing of Poultry" writes: "The Dorking is so highly prized by the English people because they know their flesh is good for the table.—In fact, by the color of its skin, their form, and the fineness of their bones, they show a great aptitude to fatten, the fat they acquire spreads itself well, and covers all parts of the body—fattened, they resemble an oval shaped ball of grease, very white, almost like Mother of Pearl from the fineness of the skin."

Dr. Eben Wight, of Boston, says: "So far as my ex

perience has gone, the Dorkings are *decidedly* the best breed for laying; the eggs come abundantly, and are of the largest size, except when they have been bred in-and-in too much."

In fact, this breed of fowl can not be bred in-and-in like other breeds, and such is the greatest drawback to breeding them in this country, unless a fresh-imported cock be introduced almost yearly amongst the hens. Many breeders of Dorkings, fearing almost total ruin in their chicken department, introduced a game cock; but though he may replenish the yard with a robust stock of chickens, I am averse to any method, adopting which destroys the purity of a breed of fowls so excellent as these, and therefore can only advise this breed of poultry to be selected by those who either have the means or facilities of obtaining an imported cock at least every second year. For this reason Mr. Dixon says, after speaking of their good qualities: "With all these merits they are not found to be a profitable stock, if kept thorough-bred and unmixed. Their powers seem to fail at an early age. They are also apt to pine away and die just at the point of reaching maturity, particularly the fairest specimens—that is, the most thorough-bred, are destroyed by this malady."

The following is an extract from the Derby and Chesterfield *Reporter:* "The common sense of the public has brought back the Dorking fowl to its wonted pre-eminence. At the sale after the Metropolitan Show, and also at the Birmingham Exhibition of 1854, the Dorking fowl met with a readier sale at larger prices than any other kind. The public voice has recognized it as the bird for the English farm-yard; it is altogether the pet of John Bull, as possessing great and good qualities without ostentation and clamor. The history of our county-town records no less than three poultry sales by public auction; and, at each of those, the Dorking fowl obtained the highest bidding—

good hens selling for as much as thirty shillings (seven dollars and fifty cents) each; and further, the most successful breeders of Dorking fowls, are, at this moment, selling their eggs readily at three guineas (fifteen dollars) per dozen."

It must be borne in mind that at the time of the writing of the above, the Brahma Pootra was but little known, and though the Dorking has many fine points (especially the delicacy and flavor of its flesh and handsome appearance when presented to the gourmand), there is one fatal objection to its being reared with success by the American farmer, and which I have described above.

Mr. Trotter, who received a prize from the Royal Agricultural Society of England, for the best "Essay on Poultry," devoted only eighteen lines to the Dorking fowl and said, "this breed degenerates when removed from its native place." And as I can not believe he meant a removal from its native town to other parts of England, I must conclude he meant a removal by exportation, because he might as well attempt to declare that an Alderney cow would degenerate by a removal from the island of that name in the English Channel to the wealds of Sussex, Surrey, or Kent.

I have already stated I believe the gray or speckled Dorking to be better than the white; and as the first consideration is the breeding-stock, I would advise, in an ordinary farm-yard, to begin with twelve hens and two cocks,—the latter should agree well together.

Too much pains can not be taken in selecting the breeding-fowls. They should not only be of the best breed, but the best of the breed. I should choose them with small heads, taper necks, broad shoulders, square bodies, white legs, and well-defined, five claws. It may be well here for me to state why the speckled or gray are to be preferred to the white Dorking. They are larger, hardier, and fatten more readily; and although it may appear anomalous, it is not less true, that white-feathered poultry has a tendency to yellowness in the flesh and fat.

THE SPANISH FOWL.

It is easy to describe this beautiful and **noble race** of fowls, as no variety of color is admissible. These birds must be black throughout, richly shaded with a metallic green lustre. A purely white face is imperatively necessary to constitute a perfect specimen. Care must be taken not to mistake the ear-lobe for the face, as in the very worst samples of the bird the former will be found quite white. In a first-class bird this color must be unmixed with red spots, and extend from the insertion of the comb to the gill, and from the ear-lobe to the beak. The ear-lobe must be large, pendant, thick, and quite free from any color.

This part of the face is more developed in the cock than the hen; in fact, he has it much larger than any other fowl. It is composed of a double skin forming a sort of bag. The cock should have a large upright comb reaching the nostril. His wattle should be very large and long, his breast round and protuberant, his tail ample, his carriage noble and very upright. The combs of the hens should fall over, and, when in good condition, be large enough to hide one side of the face. Their breasts are prominent, but not so much as in the cocks; their faces very long, thin, and skinny. The points both sexes have in common, are taper blue legs, and deviating from the required line of perfection in most other fowls, they should be long.

In shape, the body should slant downwards from the neck to the tail, and narrow from the shoulders till at the ned it approaches a point. In walking they carry themselves very upright. The following precise description of this beautiful and popular variety of fowl will be appreciated by amateurs: —

BLACK SPANISH COCK.

Cocks.—*Bill*—Strong, slightly curved, and dark-colored. *Eye*—Large dark and flashing, surrounded with a *naked white skin*, extending from the base of the comb around the ears and cheeks, meeting like a cravat under the throat and terminating in the *ear-lobes*, which are ex-

ceedingly long and pendulous. If this white face is very large and well developed, it proves high breeding; the texture of the skin cannot be too fine and smooth, and if it is blushed or spotted with red, it is considered faulty.
Comb—Single and large, beginning over the nostril, and extending backwards, should stand very erect, be regularly serrated, fine in the grain and of a rich vermilion color.
Wattles—Very large, vermilion colored, hanging a good way down the neck, which is longer in this than in any other breeds. The *body* should be as deep as possible, the legs being naturally long, and depth in body from the back to the breast bone gives a better proportion to the shape, which would otherwise look scraggy. The *legs* are clean and of a dark-blue color. *Plumage*—A brilliant jet black, hackles and saddle feathers long. *Tail*—Full, rising perpendicularly from the back, and the numerous sickle feathers falling very gracefully. *Carriage*—Bold and majestic; this is of great importance in rendering these fowls handsome and attractive.

HEAD OF BLACK SPANISH COCK.

HENS.—White face not so large as that of the cock. *Comb*—Large and hanging over, it lessens very much during the moulting or *non-laying* season, and is much affected by cold. Plumage perfectly black and glossy.

They are invaluable layers, because, although they are only moderate feeders, their eggs are larger than those of any other fowl. I have seen them four and a half ounces each. They are valuable for culinary purposes, three of them being equal to five of many other breeds. They do not sit. The best time to rear them is between April and

June; and although not perhaps to be considered very delicate chickens, so far as growth is concerned, yet it is certain they do not bear a check so well as many other breeds, and it is, therefore, well to watch them, that stimulants may be given in time. They are very naked, when hatched, and are often a long time before they feather. They may be seen running about with black feathers in their wings, and scarcely any other on their bodies.

BLACK SPANISH HEN.

At this period they require to be covered warmly every night. The great mortality among chickens of this breed is between two and four weeks old. Poultry-fanciers in England strongly recommend the use of bread and ale at least twice every day, and also cooked fresh meat chopped fine.

These fowls are rather more difficult to rear than any other, but they repay for the labor. In winter they should be protected from severe exposure and freezing, which is very apt to destroy their combs and wattles, and of course their chief beauty. I have never known any of this breed to suffer from roup, but they are subject to a peculiar kind of swelled face, which comes first by the appearance of a small knob under the skin; it increases till it has run over one side of the face, and I know of no cure for it. The sex of a Spanish fowl is easily distinguished, as the cocks show their combs plainly at a month old. At this age we always look for growth in Spanish chickens, and all faulty cocks at about seven or eight weeks old should be killed. One of the greatest faults they can have, and the only one that is plainly developed at an early age, is a *drooping comb.*

The greatest merit a Spanish fowl can have is a perfectly white face; but if a cock had the best and most faultless ever seen, it would neither excuse nor palliate a drooping comb.

The chickens, and the best of them, commonly, indeed almost always, have white in the flight feathers of the wings; and if they appear when hatched with white breasts it need cause no apprehension, as it is a common thing, and they will become black.

Lovers of these fowls have called them, says Bailey, "the Aristocracy of poultry." Fine specimens realize high prices in England. I have known one hundred dollars to be ineffectually offered for a cock and two hens. Our best Spanish fowl were formerly got from Holland, but the great demand for them, both here and in England, has nearly exhausted the market there.

In the habits of the Spanish fowl there is nothing peculiar to require notice. They are not, it is true, so quiet and disinclined to roaming as the Cochin, but if well fed at home, they will not be found to stray far from their walk. To those who desire to eat eggs, but are obliged to class chickens amongst unattainable luxuries, I would advise to adopt Spanish, as they are "everlasting layers," but "non-sitters."

THE GAME FOWL.

Among the Greeks and Romans, the pugnacious propensities and indomitable courage of animals, whether quadrupeds or birds, never failed to attract attention. The Romans, indeed, whose passion for the combats of the amphitheatre was notorious, collected not only the ferocious tenants of the Libyan desert for the gratification of their blood-thirsty disposition, but bred up dogs for the arena, and even sent authorized officers into Britain for the purpose of securing those terrible mastiffs for which the island was so celebrated, and it cannot be supposed that the combativeness of the game-cock would be overlooked. Cock-fighting was as much in vogue in Greece and Italy in ancient days, as it was during the last century in Great Britain, and is at present in India, China, Malacca, and the adjacent islands of Sumatra and Java, etc. The Greeks produced several renowned breeds of game-fowls, and Media and Persia produced others of first-rate excellence. On Cæsar's arrival in England he found the fowl domesticated; but these, as well as the hare, were forbidden as food, as it was not deemed lawful to eat them, and were only bred for the sake of fancy and pleasure. But it is probable we owe the game-fowl to the Romans, for when Britain was a Roman colony, it is not to be supposed that the Romans resident on that island would give up the sports to which they were so passionately addicted; and as they sent British fighting-dogs to Rome, so from Rome might they import their

BLACK-BREASTED RED GAME COCK.

fighting-cocks of Greek or Persian lineage. Many of us have a sort of liking for a game-cock, although we may abhor cock-fighting, and hundreds who dread their combats still cling to the breed. There are two sets of amateurs: one looks only to beauty of plumage; the other, careless of feather, scans closely those points that will tell in a fight. If fowls were not wanted for the table, and if perfect symmetry, beautiful color, hardihood, and daring were all that was required of them, the amateur might possess duckwings, (pied), or black-breasted reds, or any other of the numerous varieties of this breed, and rest content. He would, indeed, be obliged to limit the number of his pets, because the males will not agree; and unless the young cocks are looked upon with pride as those that are to figure in a main, there is always sadness in seeing sprightly ones growing up, because it is certain they must be got rid of in some way, or they will fight among themselves till but two or three remain. Nor is this propensity confined to cocks; high-bred hens are quite as pugnacious, and fatal contests between them are things of common occurrence.

The game-cock is of bold carriage; his comb is single, bright red, and upright; his face and wattle of a beautiful red color; the expression of countenance fearless, but without the cruelty of the Malay; the eye very full and bright; the beak strong, curved, well fixed in the head, and very stout at the roots. The breast should be full, perfectly straight; the body round in hand, broad between the shoulders, and tapering to the tail, having the shape of a flat-iron, or approaching heart-shaped; the thighs hard, short, and round; the leg stout; the foot flat and strong, and the spur not high on the leg. The wings are so placed on the body as to be available for sudden and rapid springs. The feathers should be hard, very strong in quills, and like the Malay it should seem as though all their feathers were **glued together till they feel like one.**

A game-cock should be what fanciers call "clever." **Every proportion should** be in perfect harmony; **and the bird, placed** on his breast in the palm of the hand, should **exactly balance.**

This is another breed of fowl where any deviation from perfection is fatal. **It has been well said, "a perfect one is not too** good, **and therefore an imperfect one** is not good **enough."** Abundant plumage, long soft hackles and saddles, too much **tail or a tail carried** squirrel-fashion over the back, the least deviation from straightness of the breast-bone, long thighs, in-knees, weak **beaks, or coarse** heads, are all **faults,** and should be avoided. These birds are generally **" dubbed "** before they **are shown at** fairs or exhibitions. **This should** be neatly performed; **every superfluous piece** of skin and flesh being removed, **so that** the head should stand out of the hackle as though it **were** shaven. The plumage should also **be so scanty that the shape of the bird,** especially the tapering of the back and **the roundness of** the body, **may be seen.** Every feather should feel as if made of whalebone, and, if raised with the finger, should **fall into its original place.** It should be almost **impossible to ruffle the** plumage of a game-**cock.** The tail should be rather **small** than otherwise, and be carried **somewhat drooping.** The plumage of these birds is trimmed before they fight. This is called "cutting out," and the less there is to remove in the way of feather the better for the bird. They **are in every respect fighting birds, and every one who sees a set-to between two of them must look on with pleasure, if it occurs as they pass through a yard.** The hens should be like **the cocks,** allowing **for difference of sex;** the necks and heads fine, legs taper, plumage hard, and combs small, upright and serrated. Hens should **not be chosen** with large or loose

3*

combs, and they should handle as hard as the cocks.

A word or two may not be out of place as to the table-properties of this beautiful breed. It is true they are in no way fit for the fattening-coop; they cannot bear the extra food without excitement, and that is not favorable to obesity. Nevertheless, they have their merits. If they are allowed to run semi-wild in the woods, to frequent sunny banks and dry ditches, they will grow full of meat, though with little fat. They must be eaten young, and a game-pullet four or five months old, caught up wild in this way and killed two days before she is eaten, is, perhaps, the most delicious chicken there is in point of flavor.

The classes into which the game fowls are divided are: black-breasted red, brown-red, duckwings, and other grays and blues, white and pieds, and black, and brassy-winged, and shawl-necks, or what are sometimes called Irish grays, which are of the largest class.

Among all the varieties of the game-fowls, the precedence must be given to that variety known as "Lord Derby's breed," which have been kept and bred with great care for upwards of one hundred years, at Knowlsley, and still maintain their high reputation. The following is a description of the cock of that breed: he is of a good round shape, well put together; has a fine long head; long and strong neck; wings large and well quilled; back short; belly round and black; tail black and sickled, being well tufted at the root; legs rather long, with white feet and nails; plumage, deep, rich red and maroon; and breast and thighs black. The Derby red hens possess little of their consort's brilliancy of feather; their body is brown, each feather-shaft being light; the breast and hackle being also light.

The Duckwings are among the most beautiful of all game-fowls. The cocks vary in the color of their hackle, saddle and breast feathers; the hackle-feathers of some strains being nearly white, in others yellow; while with some again, the breasts are black, with some streaky, and with some gray.

To breed fancy, streak-breasted brown red cockerels, mate a streaky-breasted hen to a black-red cock; nine times out of ten the cockerels will resemble the hen in color. To breed pullets to match, the cock must be streaky-breasted, and the hen black-breasted red; these will be brown-breasted reds. To obtain Duckwings, breed from a light gray-backed and winged hen, with silver hackle and salmon breast, and a black-breasted red cock; the hen should not have the slightest shade of red on the wing; this is fatal.—To obtain similar pullets, the cock must be Duckwing and the hen black-red. Pieds are bred from a white cock and black-red hen.

The color of the eggs of the game-hen varies from a dull white to a fawn. They are good layers, as many as twenty-four eggs being constantly laid by them, before they manifest a desire to sit.

As sitters, game-hens have no superiors. Quiet on their eggs, regular in the hours of coming off and returning to their charge, and confident, from their fearless disposition, of repressing the incursions of any intruder, they rarely fail to bring off good broods. Hatching accomplished, their merits appear in a still more conspicuous light. Ever on their guard, not even the shadow of a bird overhead, or the approach of man or beast, but finds them ready to do battle for their offspring; and instances have been known where rats and other vermin have thus fallen before them.

MALAY COCK.

THE MALAY FOWL.

This is another of the Asiatic breed, supposed to come from the islands of **Sumatra or Java**, and, though formerly much fancied and sought after, has of late years been suffered to decline. It has fallen before the spirit of utility; it was not useful, and it has lost ground. It is a long rather than a large bird, standing remarkably upright, falling in an almost uninterrupted slope from the head to the insertion of the tail, which is small and drooping, having very beautiful but short sickle-feathers. It has a hard, cruel expression of face, a bold eye, pearled around the edge of the lids, a hard, small comb, scarcely so long as the head, having much the appearance of a double comb trimmed very small and then flattened; a red, skinny face, very strong curved beak, and the space for an inch below it on the throat destitute of feathers. It has long yellow legs, quite clean; it is remarkable for very hard plumage, and the hinder-parts of the cock look like those of a game-cock trimmed for fighting. The hen is of course smaller than the cock. She has the same expression of face, the same curious comb; and in both sexes the plumage should be so hard that when handled it should feel as though one feather covered the body. From this cause the wings of the hen are more prominent than in other fowls, projecting something like those of a carrier-pigeon, though in a less degree. It is a beauty in the birds if the projection or knobs of flesh at the crop, on the end wing joint, and at the top of the breast are naked and red. They are good layers and sitters; their eggs have a dark shell, and are said to be superior in flavor to any other.

The chickens feather slowly, on which account no brood should be hatched after July; otherwise the cold and variable weather of autumn comes upon them before they are half grown, and the increase of their bodies has so far outstripped that of their feathers, that they are half naked about the neck and shoulders, which renders them extremely susceptible of wet and cold. The chickens are not difficult to rear; but are gawky, long-legged creatures until they have attained their full growth, and then fill out.

The original colors were, cocks of a bright, rich red,

with black breast; and hens of a bright chocolate or cinnamon color, generally one entire shade, but in some instances the hackles were darker than the rest of the plumage. Some beautiful white specimens have lately been introduced, and a few years ago there was a handsome breed of them colored like pied games.

The Malays have one great virtue; they will live anywhere; they will inhabit a back yard of small dimensions; they will scratch in the dust-pit and roost in a coal-hole, and yet lay well and show in good condition when requisite.

The Malays are inveterate fighters, and this is the quality for which they are chiefly prized in their native country, where cock-fighting is carried to the extent of excessive gambling. Men and boys may be frequently met, each carrying his favorite bird under his arm, ready to set to work the moment the opportunity shall offer.

The general character of these birds is vindictive, cruel, and tyrannical.

THE COCHIN-CHINA FOWL.

The record of the Cochin-China Fowls will always form an important chapter in the history of poultry. They were introduced in the year 1845, and were first possessed by Queen Victoria, and soon after became known and popular. They were scarce, and this made people anxious to possess them. Men became frantic after Cochin-China fowls, and this went on at an increasing ratio until the prices paid became ridiculous; a hundred good Cochins would purchase a small farm, and a cock and two hens, from favorite strains, were thought cheap if bought for less than two hundred and fifty dollars. They have, however, after fluctuating in value more than anything except railroad shares, fallen in price, for prices were unnaturally enhanced. They are now within the reach of all, and favorites with the public.

COCHIN CHINA COCK AND HEN.

The Cochin-China Cock is a bold, upright bird, with erect, indented single comb rising from the beak over the 'nostril, projecting over the neck, and then slanting away underneath to allow the root to be fixed on the top of the head. The beak is strong and curved, the eye bold, the face red, the wattle pendant, and the ear-lobe very long, hanging much lower than in other fowls. He is a bird of noble carriage, and differs from most other fowls in the following points: He has little tail; indeed, in very fine specimens, it may be said they have none; they have the hackle large and long; it falls from the neck to the back, and from its termination there is a small, gradual rise, to where the tail should be, but where its apology, some glossy, slightly twisted feathers, fall over like those of an ostrich. The next peculiarities of these birds are what are technically called "the fluff" and "the crow." The former is composed of beautifully soft, long feathers, covering the thighs till they project considerably, and garnishing all the hinder parts of the bird in the same manner; so much so that to view the widest part of the Cochin-China cock, you must look at him behind. His crow is to the crow of other cocks what the railway whistle is to to that of the errand-boy in the streets; it is loud, hoarse, and amazingly prolonged. They seem to delight in it, and will continue it till they are on tiptoe, and are compelled to exchange their usual erect position for one in which the neck is curved, and the head brought down to the level of the knees. The pullet has most points in common with the cock; her head is beautiful; the comb small, very upright, with many indentations; the face, if I may use the term, intelligent. Her body is much deeper in proportion than that of the cock; her fluff is softer, having almost a silky texture; her carriage is less erect. She has none of the falling feathers at the tail, but the little she has is upright, and should come to a blunt point, nothing like the regular rounded tails of other hens. In both, the legs should be yellow, and well feathered to the toes; flesh colored legs are admissible, but green, black, or white are defects. In buying them avoid long tails, clean legs, fifth toes, and double combs above all, take care the cock has not, nor ever has had,. sickle feathers.

The colors are buff, lemon, cinnamon, grouse, partridge, white and black; they are very good layers, laying at a certain age, without any regard to weather or time of year, beginning soon after they are five months old. The snow may fall, the frost may be thick on your windows when you first look out on a December morning, but your Cochins will provide you eggs.

They do not loose their qualities as they get older, but they lose their beauty sooner than any other, and every year seems to increase the difficulty of moulting. The age of beauty in a Cochin-China fowl is from nine to eighteen months. After this the hens become coarse; their feathers grow with difficulty; their fluff is a long time coming, and the beautiful, intelligent head is exchanged for an old, care-worn expression of face. The tails of the cocks increase as they get older.

Mr. Stretch, the eminent Cochin fancier, in writing to Mrs. Ferguson Blair, authoress of "The Hen Wife," says: —"This breed has a great disposition to accumulate abdominal fat, and consequently their food should not be of too rich a quality. Those who feed Indian meal or corn, (which contains about 8 per cent. of oily matter) have frequent cases of apoplexy among their poultry. Boiled potatoes should form a great portion of their daily food. There is another reason why Cochins should not be kept in too high condition; the eggs of such seldom produce chickens, and in a short time barrenness ensues."

Too much cannot be said in favor of their gentleness and contented disposition; a fence four feet high suffices to keep them from wandering, and they allow themselves to be taken from their perch and replaced, to be handled, exhibited, or made any use of, without the least opposition. They are also most valuable in a yard as layers during the winter months, and sitters early in the year. They are broody when others are beginning to lay.

HAMBURG FOWLS.

It is not definitely known where this breed of fowl originated; some assign its origin to Hamburg or vicinity, others to Holland. The pencilled Hamburg fowl is a beautiful bird. There are two sorts, the golden and the silver; they differ in one respect only, the fundamental color of one is white and the other a brown yellow; one description will serve for both. They have bright double combs, which should be firmly fixed on the head, inclining to neither side, nor even being loose, ending in a point which should turn upwards; clear hackles, either white or yellow; taper blue legs, and ample tails; bodies and tails accurately pencilled with black everywhere except the neck. The more correct the marking, the more valuable the bird. Their carriage is gay and proud; their shape is symmetrical, and their appearance is altogether indicative of cheerfulness, and carries an air of enjoyment which always prepossesses one in their favor.

The plumage of the cocks differs somewhat from the hens. They are very little speckled, if at all, except while chickens, when the wings and hinder parts are marked; but this seldom lasts after the first month. In the silver variety the cock is almost white, having sometimes a chestnut patch on the wing, and towards the tail some black spots, but these disappear as he gets older. The tail should be black and the sickle-feathers tinged with a reddish white; while, in the golden cock, they should be shaded with a rich bronze or copper. The cock of the golden variety is red all over, and must have well defined white deaf-ears.

No fowls require more watching than these, if it be desired to breed them for exhibition. Degeneracy shows itself in the cocks either by the black tail, or one in which white or silver predominates, or by the absence of the white deaf-ear—all these must be fatal to success. In the hens it is apparent in spotted hackles, and in patchy plumage. The delicate and distinct pencilling is lost, and a cloudy, uneven mixture takes its place. This is fatal to them as first-class birds.

The great virtue and merit of these fowls are, they are prodigious layers; and this is not brought about by any undue feeding; it is their nature. They are said never to sit, and as a rule it is true of them; but one in a thousand deviates from it. And then only when they have a run through grounds covered with wood, thereby clearly demonstating the fact that artificial life has impaired their sitting powers—originally they must have hatched their eggs like other fowls. They are excellent guards in the country; for, when disturbed in their roosting-place, they are the noisiest of the noisy, and nothing but death or liberty will induce them to hold their peace. In these, as in other birds, erroneous ideas and names have crept in; some being correct descriptions of the same fowl under another name, but others being imaginative, so far as real Hamburg fowls are concerned.

The Bolton grays and bays, and Chitteprats are identical with the Hamburg; they were also called Turkish and Creoles, which were the same as a general rule, it may be observed. No true-bred Hamburg fowl has top-knot, single comb, white legs, any approach to feather on the legs, white tail, or spotted hackle.

POLAND FOWLS.

The original Poland fowls were black, with white topknots, and gold and silver spangled. There was formerly a breed of white, with black top-knot, but that is lost. There are now, white, black and spangled. The crest of the Poland cock should be composed of straight feathers, something like those of a hackle or saddle; they should grow from the center of the crown, and fall over outside, forming a circular crest. That of the hen should be made up of feathers growing out, and turning in at the extremity, till they form a large top-knot, which should in shape resemble a cauliflower. It should be as nearly round as possible, and firm. The largest top-knots are often made up of loose feathers, that give it an uneven appearance. Now, however large these may be, they cannot compare or compete with symmetrical and firm, though smaller ones; the carriage is upright, and the breast more protuberant than in any other fowl save the Sebright Bantam; the body is very round and full, slightly tapering to the tail, which is carried erect, and which is ample, spreading towards the extremity in the hen, and having well-defined sickle-feathers; in the cock, the legs should be lead-colored or black, and rather short than otherwise. In the black variety there should be no white feathers, save in the top-knot; in that it is desirable there should be no black ones, but I have never yet seen any without them. It is a very common practice to cut them off close to the skin, so that it appears perfect, but at the first moult they re-appear.

In the golden and silver varieties, the spangling of the feathers should be black, and as correct and regular as possible; the ground-color should be rich golden tint in the one, and frosted silver in the other. In both cocks and hens the wings should be laced; each feather should have

SILVER-SPANGLED AND BLACK POLAND FOWLS.

a black marking running the length of it, and when the wing is closed, it should show three or four stripes, terminated on each feather by a distinct hackle. There exists a difference of opinion as to the marking of the breasts of the cock; some like it dark, others spangled; English fanciers prefer the latter. Spangled varieties should have top-knots the same color as the fowls; every feather should be laced like those of the Sebright Bantam, although it is very difficult to obtain them quite so distinct, many showing white feathers, which increase as the birds grow older.

In the cocks of the black breed, with white top-knots, gills are allowed, but no combs. For golden and silver spangled, neither combs nor gills, nor even the least spikes, can be tolerated. These birds are very subject to deformity, and crooked backs are common among them. The amateur who wishes to purchase will do well, when he holds the birds in his left hand, to lay the palm of his right flat on its back. In passing it gently down he will often detect one hip higher than the other, or he will find a curve in the backbone from the hips to the tail. . As these are transmitted to their offspring, and it is often difficult to get good crosses, such birds should always be rejected.

BANTAMS.

Bantams have long been favorites; their small size, their beauty, and their impudence gaining them admirers. Many years since, only those that were feathered to the toes were admired. The late John Sebright, by much attention and a thorough knowledge of the subject, succeeded in producing birds of surpassing beauty and symmetry. Those that bear this name are the most appreciated by fanciers. They are of two colors, gold and silver; they must have double combs, with pointed end and rising upwards, and well-seated on the head, firmly fixed, not inclining to one side, nor yet raised on a fleshy pedestal; laced feathers, each being edged with black; blue legs, without even the sign of a feather on them; upright tail, tipped with black at the point, which must be round and equal in width to the widest part of the feather; there should not be even a tendency to a curve in it. The side tail-feathers rising from the back to the tail should also be flat, round-topped and accurately laced. There must not be any hackle or saddle. These are the principal points of the male. The hen requires the same comb, the same accurate lacing, the prominent breast, drooping wing; her head should be very small, beak sharp. The carriage of these birds should resemble that of a good Fantail pigeon; the head and tail should be carried up in the strut of the bird, till they nearly meet, and the wing should drop down the side, instead of being carried up. In both sexes the wing-feathers should be tipped with black, and even the long feathers laced. Like all other first-class birds, these are difficult to get; and lest amateurs should be discouraged, I may almost venture to say, a faultless bird is hardly to be found. From the best-bred parents, single-combed chickens will constantly appear, but these will again produce perfectly double-combed progeny. Such are, however, only to be trusted, when the possessor of them is sure that, although defective themselves, their parents were faultless in this particular. It is never advisable to breed from a faulty bird, if a perfect one can be obtained. Small size is a *desideratum* in these fowls. They are, therefore, seldom bred early, as growth is not desired. July is early enough to hatch them. Perfect cocks should not weigh more than seventeen ounces, nor hens more than fourteen.

GAME BANTAMS.   WHITE FEATHER-LEGGED BANTAMS.   SILVER SPANGLED SEABRIGHTS.

GROUP OF BANTAM FOWLS.

Other Bantams, to pretend to excellence, should be diminutive as the Sebright, and should have the same arrogant gait; but they differ, inasmuch as the males should be large cocks in miniature, with hackle, saddle, and fully developed tail. The rule of comb is not so imperative. In black and white birds it should be double; but it is not so necessary, nor does the substitution of a single one cause disqualification. In the black breeds, white deaf-ears are necessary to excellence; and in these and the white the sickle-feathers should be long and well carried. Feathered-legged Bantams may be of any color. The old-fashioned birds were very small, falcon-hocked, and feathered with long quill-feathers to the extremity of the toe. Many of them were bearded—they are now very scarce. The Bantams are good layers, sitters and mothers, and easily reared.

THE LEGHORN FOWLS.

Within a few years past fowls, known as Leghorns, have attained some considerable notoriety—so far as I am aware, they are entirely unknown among the poultry fanciers of Great Britain, and for my own part I have been led to avoid breeding them, from the impression, be it well or ill-founded, that the characteristics were not sufficiently established to enable one to breed them true to feather and points, and to entitle them to consideration as a distinct breed. However, since the publication of the first edition of this little book, I am convinced that fowls, which have gained so fast in public favor, must have something to recommend them, and may at least be commended as worthy the attention of breeders.

Their uniform characteristics, as I at present view them, are these:—

4

Medium size, persistent as layers, being poor sitters or non-sitters, having fair fattening qualities, and very good flesh. They are besides hardy, suffering from severe weather much less than the Spanish. With this breed they are evidently closely allied, having all single combs, large white ear-lobes, and in many cases partly white faces, and in the best specimens something of the style of that justly favorite breed.

There have been several importations of the common fowls of Leghorn and its vicinity, made of late. These birds are of all colors, except black; the light colors prevailing, and they have none of the marks of a pure breed, although they possess to a greater or less degree the prevailing characteristics just given. These are called Leghorns, and are to be distinguished from the *white Leghorns*, which, in the hands of some fancies, have some claim to being well bred.

THE WHITE LEGHORNS.

These are hardy, medium-sized fowls of a quiet disposition, persistent layers, of a pure white color (though in most flocks occasional colored feathers make trouble,) with prevailingly yellow legs (flesh-colored and slate colored legs occurring now and then.) They lay a smaller egg than the Spanish, but are said to mature earlier and to be superior for the table. The white color at least makes pin-feathers less noticeable in young fowls when prepared for market. The cocks have large single combs, which should be perfectly erect, full wattles and large white ear-lobes, the white extending sometimes upon their face. The hens have delicate combs, usually large, and generally lopping like those of Spanish hens. Their wattles are also large, and their ear-lobes white.

There is certainly here a foundation for the production

of a fine breed, and if those who breed them in numbers will carefully adopt a system of points to breed for perfection in,—such points as their characteristics obviously suggest—they will surely maintain their present popularity, and establish a beautiful and useful breed.

No bird that shows any thing but "the white feather" should be used for breeding stock; nor should one, whose legs are of any but a yellow color, or whose chickens do not come true. No cock with a small drooping or crooked comb, or with colored ear-lobes, or with craven carriage or lacking in beauty, symmetry, size, style, constitution or vigor, should be kept in the yard. No hen should be kept which does not exhibit all useful characteristics, together with the drooping comb and white ear-lobes, quiet demeanor, and the laying and non-sitting qualities of the breed.

FRENCH BREEDS OF FOWLS.

Within the last two or three years some valuable importations of new breeds of poultry have been made into England and lately into the United States, from France. They have become sufficiently known and appreciated to demand our attention; and, in giving a notice of them (which I do now more fully than in my first edition, by reason of the great interest already exhibited concerning them.) I admit my obligation to the excellent work published by Mr. Ch. Jacque, in Paris, entitled "Le Poulailler," which enables me to give many details that would otherwise be wanting, and which are fully corroborated by Mr. Geo. K. Geyeline, in his "Poultry Breeding in a Commercial Point of View." [See Appendix.]

GROUP OF FRENCH FOWLS.
LA FLECHE. HOUDAN. CREVECŒUR.

THE HOUDAN.

This bird has short thick legs, and a round, well-proportioned body, large head, small top-knot, falling backward. It is bearded, and has five toes on each foot. It is a good-sized fowl, weighing, when fully grown—cock, 6 lbs.; hen, from 4½ to 5 lbs. The plumage should be speckled, white, black, and straw color. The comb is the most remarkable part of this bird; and I can not do better than quote my before-named authority: " Comb, triple, transversely in the direction of the beak, composed of two flattened spikes, of long and rectangular form, opening from right to left like two leaves of a book, thick, fleshy, and irregular at the edges. A third spike grows between these two, having somewhat the shape of an irregular strawberry, and the size of a long nut. Another, quite detached from the others and about the size of a pea, should show between the nostrils and above the beak." This gives the bird a grotesque appearance, and there is an air of impudent drollery and humor about him that is peculiar to the breed. The legs are dark leaden grey. In this breed the hens approach more nearly the weight of the cock than is usual. The hen is bearded and top-knotted, the latter appendage almost concealing the eyes. These are very popular, both as layers and as table-fowls.

HEAD OF HOUDAN COCK.

THE CREVECŒUR.

This is better known than any of the French fowl; it is one of the best layers, not only on account of number, but also of the size of the eggs, being equal in this respect to the Spanish. It is a short-legged breed, square-bodied, deep-chested, well shaped for the table.

Like most of these breeds, it is bearded and top-knotted, but the latter appendage is not like that of the Poland. It is more like a crest, and allows room in front for the

CREVECŒUR COCK.

comb. This is singularly shaped, and I shall again quote Mr. Jacque: "Comb various, but always forming two horns; sometimes parallel, straight and fleshy, sometimes joined at the base, slightly notched, pointed, and separating at their extremities; sometimes adding to this latter description interior ramifications like the horns of a young deer." The same author says: "The comb, shaped like horns, gives the Crevecœur the appearance of a devil." The legs should be black, or very dark slate blue. The plumage should be entirely black, with bright blue and metallic lustre, except the feathers of the belly, which are dark-brown. The top-knot, as in Polands, will become partly white, after moulting two or three times. Mrs. Ferguson Blair says, she has bred these birds largely and continues to do so, which is a sure proof of the consideration of which she thinks this variety worthy.

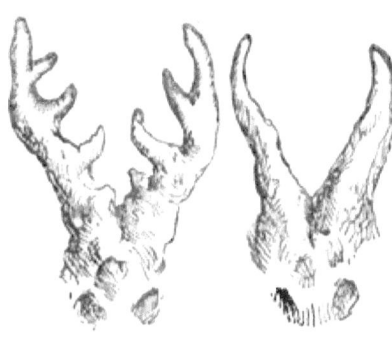
COMBS OF CREVECŒUR COCKS.

Many have their hackles, saddles, and wing-coverts straw color. These are not less pure, and they will breed black chickens; but they are less esteemed by very particular amateurs. The hens should weigh from 5 lbs. to 6 lbs. each; the cock, 7 lbs. to 7½ lbs. Just as the Houdan has a roguish air and deportment, so the Crevecœur is staid, solemn, and grave.

LA FLECHE.

This is singular bird, and no description will serve better than that of Mr. Jacque; "A strong, firm body, well seated on its legs, and long muscular feet. Appearing less than it really is, because the feathers are close; every muscular part well developed; black plumage. The La Fleche is the tallest of all French cocks; it has many points of resemblance with the Spanish, from which I believe to be descended, by crossing with the Crevecœur. It has white, loose, and transparent skin; short, juicy, and delicate flesh, which puts on fat easily. As layers they are superior, like the Crevecœur, to any breed except the Spanish; but yet, for table use, they are not as good as the Dorking.

The La Fleche has the body of the Spanish placed on legs that are forward, being immediately under the breast rather than the body of the bird. It has a bold, cheerful, lively face; but the general impression is curious from the extraordinary comb, which I will describe from M. Jacque: " Transversly double, forming two horns bending forward, united at their base, divided at their summits; sometimes even and pointed, sometimes having ramifications on the inner sides. A little combling protrudes from the upper part of the nostrils; and, although hardly as large as a pea, this combling, which surmounts the sort of rising formed by the protrusion of the nostrils, contributes to the singular aspect of the head. This measured prominence of the comb seems to add to the characteristic depression of the beak, and gives the bird a likeness to a rhinoceros."

COMB OF LA FLECHE.

It should have a large deaf-ear, perfectly white, not so large as the Spanish, but larger than that of any other fowl, slate-blue legs, darker or lighter according to age, turning to a spotted grey as they get old. The hen differs from the cock by having a smaller comb; she must have a white ear-lobe. These are a peculiar but a stylish breed; they are very good layers, and the chickens are easy to rear.

THE DOMESTIC TURKEY,

BREEDING AND MANAGEMENT.

The domestic turkey can scarcely be said to be divided, like the common fowl, into distinct breeds; although there is indeed considerable variation in color, and also in size. The finest and strongest turkeys are said to be those of a bronzed black, resembling as closely as possible the original stock; they are reared the most easily, are large, and fatten rapidly. Some turkeys are of a coppery tint, others of a delicate fawn color, others parti-colored gray and white, and some few of a pure snowy white. All these are considered inferior to the black; their color indicates something like degeneracy of constitution, and they are seldom very large-sized.

To describe the domestic turkey is superfluous; the voice of the male, the changing colors of the skin of the head and neck; his proud strut, with expanded tail and lowered wings jarring on the ground; his irascibility, readily excited by red or scarlet colors, are characteristics with which all are conversant. Turkey-cocks are pugnacious and vindictive, and often ill-treat the hens; they have been known to attack children; and combats between them and the game-cock have taken place, in which the latter was more oppressed by the weight of his antagonist than by gladiatorial skill; in fact, the bulky hero has usually been worsted, as he cannot use his spurs with the address exhibited by the game-cock, which, moreover, fights with method.

The adult turkey is extremely hardy, and bears the cold of our winter with impunity; during the severest weather, flocks will roost at night upon the branches of tall trees, preferring such accomodation to an indoor dormitory.

BRONZE TURKEY GOBBLER.

The impatience of restraint and restlessness of the turkey render it unfit company for fowls in their roosting-places; in fact, the fowl-house is altogether an improper place for these large birds, which require open sheds and high perches, and, altogether, as much freedom as is consistent with their safety. Although turkeys will roost, even during the winter months, on trees, this should by no means be allowed; the feet of the birds are apt to become frozen from such exposure to the air. It must be remembered that the domestic turkey, hardy as it is when adult, is not equal in point of endurance to its wild relative, bred in the woods and inured to the elements. Turkeys are fond of wandering about hedgerows and the borders of fields; they love to visit turnip-fields, where, besides the leaves of turnips, which they relish, they find insects, slugs, etc., which they greedily devour.

In the morning they should have a good supply of grain, and after their return from their peregrinations, another feed; by this plan not only will the due return home of the flock be insured, but the birds will be kept in good condition, and ready at any time to be put upon fattening diet.

In the choice of birds for stock, care is requisite. The cock should be vigorous, broad in the breast, clean in the legs, with ample wings and a well-developed tail-plumage; his eyes should be bright, and the carunculated skin of the neck full and rapid in its changes of color. The hen should be like the cock in plumage; those with white feathers appearing amidst the black should be rejected; her figure should be plump, and her actions lively and animated. The hen breeds when a year old, or rather in the spring succeeding that in which she herself left the egg; but she is not in her prime until the age of two or three years, and will continue for two or three years more in full constitutional vigor.

About the middle of March, generally speaking, the female commences laying; she indicates the coming event by a peculiar cry, by strutting about with an air of self-satisfaction, and often by prying into out-of-the-way places, evidently in quest of a secret spot for incubation; for the instinctive dread of the male is not removed by domestication, nor has the male lost that antipathy to the eggs which is his characteristic in a state of nature. She should now be closely watched, and some management is required to induce her to lay in the nest assigned to her. The nest should be prepared of straw and dried leaves; it should be secluded; and to excite her to adopt it, an egg, or a piece of chalk cut into the form of an egg, should be placed in

BRONZE HEN-TURKEY.

it. When her uneasiness to lay is evident, and symptoms prove that she is ready, she should be confined in the shed, barn, or place in which her nest (which should be a wicker basket) is prepared, and let out as soon as the egg is laid. The turkey-hen is a steady sitter; nothing will induce her to leave her nest; indeed, she often requires to be removed to her food, so overpowering is her instinctive affection. The hen should on no account be rashly disturbed, no one except the person to whom she is accustomed, and from whom she receives her food, should be allowed to go near her, and the eggs should not be meddled with. On about the twenty-sixth day, the chicks leave the eggs, and these, like young fowls, do not require food for several hours. It is useless to cram them as some do, fearing lest they should starve. When the chicks feel an inclination for food, nature directs them how to pick it up. There is no occasion for alarm if for many hours they content themselves with the warmth of their parent and enjoy her care only. Yet some food must be provided for them, and this should be of course suited to their nature and appetite; here, too, let the simplicity of nature be a guide.

The first diet offered to turkey-chicks should consist of eggs boiled hard and finely mixed, or curd with bread-crumbs and the green part of onions, parsley, etc., chopped very small and mixed together so as to form a loose, crumby paste; oatmeal with a little water may also be given. They will require water; but this should be put into a very shallow vessel, so as to insure against the danger of the chicks getting wet. Both the turkey-hen and her chickens should be housed for a few days; they may then, if the weather be fine, be allowed a few hours' liberty during the day, but should a shower threaten, they must be put immediately under shelter. This system must be persevered in for three or four weeks. By this time they will have acquired considerable strength, and will know how to take care of themselves. As they get older, meal and grain may be given more freely. They now begin to search for insects and to dust their growing plumage in the sand. At the age of about two months, or perhaps a little more, the males and females begin to develop their distinctive characteristics.

In the young males, the carunculated skin of the neck and throat, and the contractile horn-like comb on the forehead, assume a marked character. This is a critical period. The system requires a full supply of nutriment and good housing at night is essential. Some recommend that a few grains of Cayenne pepper, or a little bruised hempseed, be mixed with their food. The distinctive sexual marks once fairly established, the young birds lose the name of "chicks," or "chickens," and are termed "turkey-poults." The time of danger is over, and they become independent, and every day stronger and more hardy. They now fare as the rest of the flock, on good and sufficient food.

With respect to the diseases of the turkey, with them as with all other poultry, prevention is better than cure. The most important rules are, let the chicks never get wet, and encourage them to eat heartily by giving a good variety of food; yet to beware of injuring the appetite by too much pampering. Taking a pride in them is the great secret of success in the rearing of domestic poultry.

THE GUINEA FOWL.

The common Guinea fowl is a native of Africa, where it appears to be extensively distributed. It frequents the open glades and borders of forests, the banks of rivers, and other localities where grain, seeds, berries, insects, etc., offer an abundant supply of food. It is gregarious in its habits, associating in considerable flocks, which wander about during the day and collect together on the approach of evening. They roost in clusters on the branches of trees or large bushes, ever and anon uttering their harsh, grating cry, till they settle fairly for the night. The Guinea fowl does not trust much to its wings as a means of escape from danger; indeed it is not without some difficulty that these birds can be forced to take to flight, and then they wing their way only a short distance, when they alight and trust to their swiftness of foot. They run with very great celerity, are shy and wary, and seek refuge amongst the dense underwood, threading the mazes of their covert with wonderful address. The female incubates in some concealed spot on the ground. Like all the gallinaceous birds, the Guinea fowl is esteemed for its flesh and its eggs, which, though smaller than those of the common fowl, are very excellent and numerous. The hen commences to lay in the month of May and continues during the entire summer. The Guinea fowl is of a wild, shy, rambling disposition; and, domesticated as it is, pertinaciously retains its original habits, and is impatient of restraint. It loves to wander along hedgerows, over meadows, through corn-fields or clover, and amidst copses and shrubberies; hence these birds require careful watching, for the hens will lay in secret places, and will sometimes absent themselves entirely from the farm-yard until they return with a young brood around them.

So ingeniously will they conceal themselves and their nest, so cautiously leave it and return to it, as to elude the searching glance of boys well used to bird-nesting; but it may always be found from the watchful presence of the cock while the hen is laying. There is one disadvantage in this—the bird will sit at a late period, and bring forth her brood when the season is too cold for the tender chickens. The best plan is, to contrive that the hen shall lay in a quiet, secluded place, and to give about twenty of the earliest eggs to a common hen ready to receive them, who will perform the duties of incubation with steadiness. In this way a brood in June can be easily obtained. The young must receive the same treatment as those of the turkey, and equal care; they require a mixture of boiled vegetables, with curds, farinaceous food, as grits, meal, etc.; they should be induced to eat as often and as much as they will. In a short time they begin to search for insects and their larvæ ; and with a little addition to such a fare as this, and with what vegetable matter they pick up, they will keep themselves in good game condition without cramming or overfeeding. For a week or two before being killed for the table they should have a liberal allowance of grain and meal. Guinea fowls mate in pairs; **overlooking this circumstance frequently occasions disappointment in the broods. The period of incubation is twenty-six days.** Though they are not unprofitable birds, as they are capable of procuring almost entirely their own living, they are rejected by many on account both of their wandering habits, which give trouble, and their disagreeable voice. The males when pugnacious, though spurless, are capable of inflicting considerable injury on other poultry with their stout, hard beaks.

Like their wild progenitors, domestic Guinea fowls prefer roosting in the open air to entering a fowl-house ; they generally choose the lower branches of some tree, or those of large thick bushes, and there congregate together in close array; before going to roost they utter frequent calls to each other, and when one mounts, the others follow in rotation. They retire early, before the common fowl.

The Guinea fowl is not so large a bird as it appears, its loose, full plumage making it seem larger than it is ; it does not, when plucked, weigh more than a common fowl. The male and female very much resemble each other ; the male, however, has the casque higher, and the wattles are of a blueish red—the wattles in the female are smaller, and red.

TOULOUSE GEESE.

THE DOMESTIC GOOSE.

The domestication of the goose, like that of the domestic fowl, is hidden in the remotest ages of antiquity. Among the Greeks and Romans, it seems to have been the only really domesticated water-fowl they possessed, and appears to have held exactly the same place in their esteem that it still retains with us after the lapse of two or nearly three thousand years.

Geese require a dormitory apart from other poultry, and a green field, or common, with a convenient pond of water—often at command in the country. Let not, however, the keeper of geese suppose that their daily grazing is sufficient for their maintenance in proper condition, as they require, in addition, a supply of grain, oats or barley, morning and evening, and with this they will do credit to their keep; many young geese, common-fed only, pine and die for want of sufficient nutriment. Dysentery attacks them, accompanied by spasms of the limbs, or cramps as it is called; this disease is aggravated by cold and wet, their impoverished system is destitute of stamina, and thus a fair flock prospering in spring, is more than decimated before autumn. In allowing geese to range at large, it is requisite to be aware that they are very destructive to all garden and farm crops, as well as to young trees, and must therefore be carefully excluded from orchards and cultivated fields.

If we traverse a pasture or common, on which geese are kept, we find the flocks of the respective owners keeping together: and if by chance they mingle on the pond or sheet of water, they separate towards evening, and retire each flock to its own domicile. On extensive commons where many thousands of geese are kept, the rule is scarcely ever broken; the flocks of young geese brought up together, as their parents were before them, form a united band, and thus distinct groups herd together, bound by the ties of habit.

Those who breed geese generally assign one gander to four or five females. In mild seasons the goose lays early. She sits with exemplary patience, but ought, during incubation, to be well supplied with food and water, placed in a convenient and undisturbed situation, to which she may have free access. The gander is very attentive to his favorite, sits by her, and is vigilant and daring in her defence.

Like young turkeys, goslings are about a month in hatching. On the first day after the goslings are hatched, they may be let out, if the weather be warm, care being taken not to let them be exposed to the unshaded heat of the sun, which might kill them, the food given is prepared

BREMEN OR EMBDEN GEESE.

with some Indian meal, coarsely ground bran, lettuce-leaves, and crusts of bread boiled in milk. To such goslings as are a little strong, this food need only be given twice a day, morning and evening, continuing to give it till the wings begin to cross on the back, and after this a larger amount of green food with a little corn, wheat, etc., morning and evening.

The principal breeds of geese are the China Goose (which is also called the Guinea Goose, Spanish Goose, African Goose, and a host of other names in the English tongue), Toulouse Goose, and the Bremen or Embden Goose.

The China Goose lays a great number of eggs, and a cross between it and the Toulouse, gives a delicious bird for the table. The goose resembles the gander in form and color, and both have dark **brown strips down** the back of the neck.—They are graceful in **form, but have** that most trying of all defects, a discordant voice, and being very loquacious, it is a serious evil to be constantly exposed to their whining, discontented harsh cry—on a *distant* piece of water they look **well, as** they are peculiarly elegant in movement. Their color is brown, shaded with white on the *breast ; bill*, tuberculated and black ; *neck*, long ; *feet* and *legs*, black.

The Toulouse Goose should be tall and erect, with the body hanging on the ground ; the *breast* and the *body* light grey ; *back*, dark grey ; *neck*, darker grey ; *wings* and *belly* should shade off to white, but there should be but little actual white visible ; *bills*, pale flesh color, hard and strong ; *legs* and *feet*, deep orange, approaching **red.** The weight of these birds by careful feeding and management has become extraordinary, 74 lbs. for three birds has been attained. The **Cup** gander at Birmingham, **in 1859,** weighed 33 lbs., and in 1860, 30 lbs.—Goslings **early in** October often weigh 20 to 22 pounds.

Bremen or Embden Geese have blossom-white plumage ; *bills*, flesh color ; *legs* and *feet*, orange. These birds attain great weights, averaging from 45 to 50 lbs. per pair, and are valuable **on account of** the superior quality and color of the down, **but to look** well they must have access to a pond. The quiet domestic character of the Bremen geese causes them to lay on flesh rapidly, they seldom stray from their homes and much of their time is spent in a state of repose.

FEEDING AND MANAGEMENT OF DUCKS.

It is not in all situations that ducks can be kept with advantage; they require water even much more than the goose; they are no graziers, yet they are hearty feeders, and excellent "snappers-up of unconsidered trifles." Nothing comes amiss to them—green vegetables, especially when boiled, the rejectamenta of the kitchen, meal of all sorts made into a paste, grains, bread, animal substances, worms, slugs and snails, insects and their larvæ, are all accepted with eagerness. Their appetite is not fastidious; in fact, to parody the line of a song, "they eat all that is luscious, eat all that they can," and seem to be determined to reward their owner by keeping themselves in first rate condition, if the chance of so doing is afforded them. They never need cramming; give them enough and they will cram themselves; yet they have their requirements and ways of their own, which must be conceded. Confinement will not do for them; an orchard, a green lane, and a pond; a farm yard, with barns and water, a common of rather wide extent, smooth and level, with a sheet of water and rice ditches, abounding in the season with tadpoles and the larvæ of aquatic insects—these are the localities in which the duck delights, and in such they are kept at little expense. They traverse the green sward in Indian file, and thus return at evening to their dormitory, or emerge from it to the edge of the pond, over which they scatter themselves, thus also they come to the call of their feeder. Ducks should always have a lodging place of their own;

they should be separated from fowls, and never housed beneath their perches; yet where fowls are kept, a little contrivance would suffice to make them a comfortable berth in a fowl-house. In winter, a thin bedding of straw, rushes, or fern leaves should be placed on the floor of their dormitory, and changed every second day. More than four or five females should not be allowed to a single drake. The duck lays a great many eggs in the season. She is chiefly a Spring layer, and while she is laying, produces an egg generally every day. The female will cover with comfort twelve or fourteen eggs, and in most cases is a steady sitter. When she inclines to sit give her a plentiful nest, with some broken hay or straw ready at hand, with which to cover the eggs when she leaves them. As nature instructs her to use this precaution, no doubt it is best to give her the opportunity. Let her be supplied with food and water directly after she leaves her nest, and if she chooses to take a bath it will do no harm. It is common to put ducks' eggs under hens, and it is ludicrous, though somewhat painful, to see the trepidation and anxiety of the foster-mother on the edge of a pond, into which the young ducks have plunged, regardless of her feelings and incessant clucking—a language they do not understand. If tame ducks visit the water too early, they are very apt to become cramped, and perish; for if they once become saturated with water, they invariably perish. Ducks never become wet when properly fledged, for their plumage throws off the fluid, and they return dry from the pond; but ducklings, while yet in the down, get wet, and should not therefore go to the water until feathers supply the place of the early down. They are easily reared, being fed on meal mixed with potatoes; they are useful in gardens, which they clear of slugs and snails, with little injury to crops of vegetables. The ponds to which they have access should contain neither pike nor eels; and rats should be extirpated from the same places. Rats and skunks often **thin** out a flock of ducklings **most** uncompromisingly.

Ducks are generally found good sitters and mothers, and it is **a pity** to rob them of a task which is more advantageously performed by them than by hens. Let the ducks **hatch** their own ducklings, only taking care to keep **her and** them from water.

WHITE AYLESBURY DUCKS.

Of all ducks, the best are the Aylesbury—plumage of unspotted white, a pale flesh-colored bill, a dark, prominent eye, **with orange** legs and a stately carriage, are the characteristics of this race, whose name is derived **from** the town of Aylesbury, England, in which neighborhood they are kept in large numbers for the supply of the London markets. The weight of the adult Aylesbury duck **should at** least average, if properly fed, from ten to twelve pounds the pair (duck and drake). Instances have, however, occurred where the drakes have come up to eight pounds and upwards, and would in all probability, if fattened, reach ten pounds each. They are prolific layers. **From two** of these ducks, **three hundred eggs have** been obtained in the course of twelve months; in addition to which one of them sat twice, the other only once, the three nests giving thirty young ones. The eggs vary in color, some being white, while others are of a pale-blue tint, the **average** weight being three ounces. As a further recommendation for them in an economical point of view, their consumption **of food** is less than that of the common duck; and another advantage may be found in their comparative silence from the continuous "quack, quack, quack," of the latter bird. They also attain greater weight in less time;

and from their superior appearance when plucked, are a far more marketable article.

The Aylesbury duck is so distinct from any other as to be easily distinguished by any person desirous of obtaining them. They are better sitters than the Rouen duck, and also, from their lighter form, better nurses than the latter. Some writers on poultry have given a preference to the Rouen duck over the Aylesbury, but I should say their opinions must be biased by the richness of the Rouen's plumage. This, however, is a point of minor consideration in a bird whose merits must be weighed by its value as an economical inhabitant of the poultry-yard; but where both these recommendations can be combined, there are few persons who would not by experience prefer the Aylesbury.

Mr. John Giles, of Woodstock, Connecticut, who has probably had as much, if not more experience in the breeding and management of fowls of all descriptions than any other fowl-fancier in the country, says of the Aylesbury duck:

"The breed I brought with me from England are white, with white bills; their flesh is of a beautiful white; their weight eight to ten pounds per pair when fully grown. They are considered a rarity in London, commanding one-third more price than any other ducks brought to market."

Mowbray says: "The white Aylesbury ducks are a beautiful and ornamental stock. They are said to be early layers and breeders. Vast quantities are fattened for the London markets, where they are in great demand. Many families derive a comfortable living from breeding and rearing ducks, the greater part of which—the early ones, at all events—are actually reared by hand. The interior of the cottages of those who follow this occupation presents a very curious appearance to the stranger, being furnished with boxes for the protection of the tender charge of the good-wife, whose whole time and attention are taken up with this branch of domestic economy."

The *American Agriculturist* says, in the number for August, 1864: "The only variety which really rivals the Rouen as a useful and economical bird is the Aylesbury. These are a pure white English variety, are beautiful birds, and highly esteemed in the markets of Great Britain, as also in the United States where they are known. They are good layers and nurses, not noisy, good feeders, and by some decidedly preferred to the Rouen."

The Field, (London,) of Dec. 26th, 1864, says: "Aylesburys are superior in weight and early maturity to Rouens, and are consequently generally preferred by those who breed for the supply of the London markets."

THE MUSK OR MUSCOVY DUCK.

The Musk Duck, so termed from the strong scent of musk which its skin exhales, is undoubtedly the type of a genus very distinct from that of the common duck. In this species the feathers are large, lax, and powdery; the cheeks are naked, and the base of the bill is carunculated. This duck greatly exceeds the ordinary kind in size, and the male is far larger than the female. The general color is glossy blue-black, varied more or less with white; but they are also known pure white and blue. A scarlet fleshy space surrounds the eye, continued from scarlet caruncles at the base of the beak. The tail is destitute of the curled feathers so conspicuous in the tail of the common drake.

According to Buffon, these birds were introduced into France from Guiana about the year 1540. The species
... Day who termed it the wood-duck of Bra-

zil. Marcgrave, who describes the Musk Duck as black with white shoulders, terms it "a woodland duck, as large as a goose." He observes it is common in Brazil, Guiana, and Paraguay. In Paraguay it is seen either in pairs or in flocks of twenty or thirty, which roost together on high trees; the female lays in September from ten to fourteen eggs, in the hollow of a tree, on a bed of feathers from the breast of the male. Mr. Eyeton, in his valuable work on the duck tribe, states that these birds "are supposed to be the original natives of South America"—an impression which evidently implies that he had not been able to verify the original locality of the species.

The Musk Duck is fond of warmth, passing the night, at the north, not in the open air, but in the fowl-house, with the cock and hens; and selecting by day the most sunny corner to bask and dose in. It will never go near the water if it can help it, but will prefer the farm-yard, the precincts of the kitchen, or even the piggery itself, to the clearest stream that ever flowed. In fact, it hates water, except some dirty puddle to drink and dabble in. It does sometimes seem to enjoy a bath; but so does a pigeon or canary-bird. Its very short leg does not appear to be mechanically adapted for the purpose of swimming. It waddles on the surface of a pond as much as it does on dry land, and is evidently out of its place in either situation. Its proper mode of locomotion is through the air; its congenial haunts being among the branches of trees.

The female of the Musk duck has considerable power of flight, and is easy and self-possessed in the use of its wings. It is fond of perching on the tops of barns, walls, etc. Its feet appear, by their form, to be more adapted to such purposes than most of other ducks. If allowed to spend the night in the hen-house, the female will generally go to roost by the side of the hens, but the drake is too heavy to mount thither with ease. His claws are sharp and long and he approaches the tribe of "scratchers," in an unscientific sense, being almost as dangerous to handle incautiously as an ill-tempered cat, and will occasionally adopt a still more offensive and scarcely-describable means of annoyance.

He manifests little affection for his partner, and none towards her offspring. The possession of three or four mates suits him and them better than to be confined to the company of a single one. He bullies other fowls, sometimes by pulling their feathers, but more frequently by following them close, and repeatedly thrusting his face in their way, with an offensive and satyr-like expression of countenance.

The Musk Duck, though a voracious feeder, is easily fattened. As layers, they are inferior to the Aylesbury or Rouen. Their eggs are rounder than those of the common duck, and frequently incline to a greenish tint.

The newly-hatched young resemble those of the common tame duck; they are covered with down, the shades of which indicate the color of the future feathers; and they do not for some time show any appearance of the tuberculated face. They are delicate, and require some care while young, but are quite hardy when full grown. Their food should be anything that is nutritious, supplied in abundance and variety. The Musk duck is excellent eating, if killed just before it is fully fledged; but it is longer in becoming fit for the table than the common duck. The flesh is at first high-flavored and tender; but an old bird would be rank, and the toughest of tough meats.

No very high opinion is entertained as regards the appearance, habits or economy of this duck in the poultry-yard. The bloated look of the head, the inordinate length of the body, its awkward legs and twaddle walk, mar the effects of colors that are often brilliant and striking.

THE ROUEN DUCK.

The Rouen Duck derives its name from the city of Rouen on the river Seine, in France, and is esteemed highly by epicures. It is a prolific bird, and lays large eggs. Its size is the criterion of its value. In color the Rouen duck closely assimilates to the wild duck; the drake's especially is magnificent; its head and neck being a rich lustrous green, with a white ring at the base of the neck; breast a reddish brown; the remainder of the body and wings partaking very much of the colors of the wild mallard. The duck is a brown bird, the feathers being all marked with black; she has, at a very early age, a great development of her "stomach pouch," which frequently hangs so low as to impede the action of the bird. From this and other causes the Rouen is a less active variety than the Aylesbury, and for the same cause does not make a good sitter, being too heavy for the young birds when hatching, and for this cause her eggs should be placed under a hen. This is the more necessary, as the duck lays so long, that it often makes the brood a very late one, if the eggs are not set till she is broody. Cases are reported of ducks of this breed, which laid an egg a day for 85 and 92 successive days, and though this is unusual, yet they often lay a similar length of time before they become ready to sit.

The Rouen is the most lethargic, and, consequently, the most speedily fed of any. Their whole appearance is rather ungainly; but the most inconsiderate observer can hardly fail of being struck with the size of good specimens of this breed. They are as hardy as any other kind, and rarely evince any disposition to wander from their home, and an especial recommendation is, that they are not noisy.

PAIR OF ROUEN DUCKS.

POULTRY FOR EXHIBITION.

There is neither so much profit, nor so much honor, in gaining prizes with bought birds as with those that have been bred at home. As a rule, those who are in a position to give the largest sums are not those who pay the most attention to their birds; and it is almost impossible one person should possess all the advantages requisite to success. The produce of the best birds in the world, if only moderately attended to, will not be better than those of merely good ones favored by every advantage. If it is wished to exhibit at early shows or fairs, say in June, July, and August, the chickens should be hatched early in February, one thing alone operates disadvantageously, namely, that the nights are longer.

About the middle of January two or three hens should be set in a warm, sheltered spot, and each should have seven eggs from selected birds, above all such as have no capital defects or lack of any virtue. Grant that five chickens are hatched under each, which is enough—and as many as she can rear,—it will take at least fifteen chickens hatched to produce six fit to show in June.

It is easy to give any quantity of food, and to supply any amount of heat, but it must always be impossible to give sufficient nourishment in eight hours to last for and carry chickens over the twenty-four. It will therefore be necessary to feed them twice after dark, and this should be done even with those that are intended for the market, and never hope for any distinction beyond that of being spring chickens and eaten with asparagus. Say that the last daylight-meal is at four o'clock, and then at eight give them another by candle light.

The coop should be in doors, covered carefully, so as to

exclude any cold air. Place a dark board, on which the food, curd, egg, or bread and milk will be easily seen, in front, and then raising a corner of the covering immediately before the board, throw down the light of a candle on it, and call the chickens. Repeat the meal at 11 o'clock, and again at 7 in the morning; and the night is reduced to eight hours' fasting, which the chickens can bear without injury. As they grow, if either of them shows any great defect, fatten it for the table or market, and reserve all that you can of those that promise to make a good return. Of course, this is only needed for those that are hatched early; the late ones do not require it, they have nature on their side, and she is a good nurse. Those very early chickens are not wanted for late shows or fairs; the produce of April or May will always beat them. Where many fowls are bred from a good stock, and kept in a farmyard affording all necessary food, we would be content to leave altogether, even though we intended to exhibit. Weight is never the principal point in fowls. It is more important in December and the later winter-shows, than it is between August and November. At this later period that which is looked for in a prize-taker is a large frame. The food has been expended in height, length, and breadth, and while this is the case there will be no weight and fat. That which stops the growth and induces fattening lessens the probability of success.

All fowls should be together for some days before they go to a show or fair. Being on the same walk is not enough; they should be daily confined in a small space. If this precaution is not taken, success is frequently marred by the pen having one hen or another torn to pieces, or eaten, at least so far as the scalp and back part of the neck are concerned. This is more frequently the work of the hens than of the cock; and when they are put together, if one begins to beat another, and is allowed to do so without resistance, it is useless to think of their agreeing, and madness to think of showing them together. As a hen or pullet is frequently spoiled for exhibition in a few minutes, it may be worth while to describe the first appearance of an intended aggression.

The pugnacious hen will begin by raising herself on tiptoe till she can look down on her antagonist, then, dropping her wings and raising her hackle, she will strike the first blow. If this be submitted to, there is no hope for the beaten. She should be removed; they will never agree, and she will be eaten. It may be asked why these things do not occur in yards. The reason is simple. Because the space allows room for the victim to escape; but it is one of the inexplicable things of poultry, that when in presence of a pugnacious mate, a hen or pullet tries no resistance, she endeavors to find an outlet for flight; failing that, she chooses a corner into which she thrusts her head, and thus "accepting the situation" she stands still while she is eaten. But without fighting they sometimes disagree, and then they show to disadvantage, because the weakest bird is always out of sight.

If an amateur who wishes to exhibit, has fifteen fowls to choose from, and to form a pen of a cock and two hens, he should study and scan them while feeding at his feet in the morning. He should then have a place similar to an exhibition pen, wherein he can place the selected birds; they should be raised to the height at which he can best see them, and before he has looked long at them defects will become apparent one after the other, till, in all probability, neither of the subjects of his first choice will go to the show. We also advise him rather to look for defects than to dwell on beauties; the latter are always prominent enough. Then pen of which we speak should be a moveable one, for convenience sake, and it is well to leave the fowls in it for a time to accustom them to each other.

In all cases (save those in which white plumage is desirable) we advise that fowls, such as Dorking, Cochins, Brahma Pootras, and all golden birds, should run at liberty till they are wanted to send away. Spanish are improved by confinement in a dark place for some days before exhibition, giving just enough of light to enable them to pick their food and to perch. They should also be littered with straw, as cleanliness has much to do with the success of these birds.

Game-fowls should be kept up for a few days, and fed on bread, meal, barley, and peas. These latter make the plumage hard, but they must be used sparingly, as they have a tendency to fatten. White feathered birds, such as Silver-pencilled Hamburgs, the top-knots of Silver Polands, the tails of Silver-spangled, all require washing. This is not difficult. Put a handful of soda in a bowl of warm water. Immerse the fowl entirely, rinse thoroughly with cold water, wipe with a flannel and place in a basket, with soft straw, before a fire to dry. All fowls should have their legs washed before they are sent to a show; scurf or dead skin should be removed from the comb, dry dirt from the beak, and stains from the plumage. Baskets in which they are packed should *always be round,* high enough for the cocks to stand upright, and covered with canvas. If a single covering of canvas is not deemed enough it may be double, and the space between filled with hay. No injury can then, by any possibility, be done to the birds. But if the basket be square, feathers must be broken, and if the top be unyielding wicker-work, whether it be a topknot or comb that comes in contact with it, it must suffer by being flattened.

Fowls should be thoroughly fed before they leave for a show, but the food should be soft. Sopped or steeped bread is excellent. Hard food is to be avoided, because the digestion is to take place without help from exercise, gravel, or anything else. This is more important than may appear at first, when it is considered they will probably undergo the ordeal of judgment within a few hours of their departure from home, and that indigestion is accompanied by sickly and ruffled plumage, dullness of color, dark comb and yellow face. In cold weather it is necessary they should have plenty of straw in their baskets for warmth sake; and when fowls go frequently to fairs or shows the straw should be renewed every time.

Fowls are not chilly, but they dislike draughts, and even in the railroad cars there are chinks and crevices through which there is an active current. They are also left in open and exposed spots at stations, and then the warm straw plays a useful part.

In fowls, as in other things, "let well alone" is a good and useful motto. When they return from a fair, looking in perfect health, do nothing; but if combs be dark, or crops be hard, a tablespoonful of castor oil is a valuable medicine and proper treatment. Where it is convenient, it is useful to have a spare run, where birds can be put down on their return from fairs, and subjected, if necessary, to an especial treatment. I do not say this is necessary, especially in the present day.

They seldom require any other treatment than purgatives to remove the accumulations of three or four days of unnatural appetite, undue feed from mistaken kindness, and perhaps rubbish from the bottoms of the cages.

These are things so generally known, it would seem ridiculous to mention them; yet I would not be justified in leaving them out. I speak of one of them when I remind exhibitors that birds in a pen must match as to comb and color of legs.

APPENDIX.

REPORT OF A VISIT TO THE POULTRY YARDS OF FRANCE.

[NOTE.—Mr. Geo. K. Geyelin, a civil engineer connected with the National Poultry Company, of Bromley in Kent, England, took occasion before erecting the extensive buildings proposed to be put up, and perhaps already erected, by the company, to visit France with a view to look into the systems pursued in raising fowls on a very large scale. He embodied his observations in a concise report to the stockholders, which is given with few omissions.]

THE OBJECT OF THE TRIP.

The primary object of the voyage was to ascertain everything connected with Poultry Breeding in France which might assist in promoting the success of our undertaking; also to inquire into the truth of numerous assertions in the public papers, that there existed in the vicinity of Paris most extensive Gallinocultural establishments, which by their particular system of artificial incubation, rearing, and feeding Poultry on horseflesh, realized in one instance, viz., in that of M. de Soras, upwards of £40,000 per annum. I need scarcely say that, after the most searching investigation within a radius of forty miles of Paris, my opinion has been fully confirmed that such establishments do not nor can possibly exist.   *   *   *

[Hearing, however, that one existed at Mouy, he telegraphed and wrote, and finally he says]: To make the inquiry triply sure, I started myself for Mouy; arrived at Reil Junction, I was informed that such an establishment really did exist at Mouy, and within half a mile of the railway station, which news delighted me, to know that my journey was not like a wild goose chase; therefore, on arriving at Mouy, I proceeded at once to the Poultry establishment, but not of M. de Soras, whose name is not even known to any person in that neighborhood, but of M. Manoury, éleveur à Angy près Mouy, to whom I briefly related the object of my call; I was received with every courtesy and informed that he knew of no such name as M. de Soras, nor of any establishment of the kind, but that he devoted his time to rearing some 5000 head of Poultry per annum; he neither fed them on horseflesh or supplied the markets of Paris, that he sold none but pure breeds, and those to gentlemen and fancy Poultry dealers; nevertheless, that his system of hatching, rearing, and feeding was so different to that adopted by others that it might possibly have given rise to those exaggerated reports; after which he conducted me over his establishment, and explained most minutely the system he has adopted, which, however, I need not explain in this part, as I shall have to refer to it under the several headings. I will now conclude by adding that I have visited all those places in France so justly famed for their Poultry, and from which those celebrated breeds of Houdan, La Flèche, and Crève Cœur are obtained, where also I met with the utmost courtesy in my inquiries, though I had been informed that the farmers never explained or showed their system of Poultry rearing to any one, which possibly may be true as regards their countrymen.

Of Artificial Incubation I have observed four different systems, which, although said to answer well, are yet far from being applicable to hatching in a commercial point of view. It matters indeed very little what system is adopted provided the heat is maintained at an even temperature: to obtain this, various regulators have been invented, but none of which can as yet dispense with personal care. They all say that their regulators are perfect if the temperature of the room can be kept at the same degree of heat during incubation, that then they can regulate the heat of the incubator to any given degree; but as such conditions of a uniform temperature are impossible to maintain, considering the variations in the temperature of the atmosphere, I consider artificial hatching too expensive for ordinary purposes, and only to be adopted at certain times of the year, and then only in establishments where the heat can be maintained at a uniform temperature, day and night, by personal care.

At the Jardin des Plantes, in Paris, the manager of the poultry department, M. Vallée, employs an apparatus of his own invention, which he has patented, and for which he has obtained prizes at two exhibitions. The principle consists of water heated by means of a lamp as a medium for hatching: the temperature is regulated by admitting more or less cold air by means of a valve opened or closed by a mercury float.

At the Jardin d'Acclimatization two systems of artificial incubation are in use, and although both are on the hot-water principle, yet they differ materially,—the one is heated by means of a lamp and the temperature regulated by a valve admitting more or less cold air, and which is effected by a piston acted upon by the expansion or condensation of air under different temperatures; the other consists merely of a zinc box covered with non-conducting materials. This apparatus requires neither lamp, regulator, or thermometer, the hot water is renewed every twelve hours, and it is said to answer admirably. The eggs are placed in a drawer underneath the water tank, but I cannot help thinking that with an atmospheric temperature at or below freezing-point, it would be very difficult to prevent the rapid cooling of the water.

The next and last system of artificial hatching I shall notice is that shown to me by M. Manoury at Mouy. It consists of an ordinary wine cask lined on the inside with plaster of Paris. In this cask several trays with eggs are suspended, and the top of the cask is provided with a certain number of vent-holes for admitting air, which is regulated by means of vent-pegs: the cask is surrounded to the top with a thickness of about four feet of horse manure. Though I am assured that this principle answers well, I entertain serious doubts about it for the same reasons as before stated.

NATURAL HATCHING differs entirely from what I ever saw before, and in some parts of France forms a special trade carried on by persons called *Couveurs* or Hatchers. These hatch for farmers at all times of the year at so much per egg, or purchase the eggs in the market and sell the chickens as soon as hatched from threepence to sixpence each, according to the season of the year. This system may aptly be called a living hatching machine, and, in my opinion, it is the very best and cheapest way of hatching, as will be seen by the following description :—

THE HATCHING ROOM is kept dark, and at an even temperature in summer and winter. In this room a number of boxes, two feet long, one foot wide, and one foot six inches deep, are ranged along the walls. These boxes are covered in with lattice or wire work, and serve for turkeys to hatch any kind of eggs. Similar boxes, but of smaller dimensions, are provided for broody fowls. The bed of the boxes is formed of heather, straw, hay, or cocoa-fibres; and the number of eggs for turkeys to hatch is two dozen, and one dozen for hens.

At any time of the year, turkeys, whether broody or not, are taught to hatch in the following manner :—Some addled eggs are emptied, then filled with plaster of Paris, then placed in a nest; after which, a turkey is fetched from the yard and placed on the eggs, and covered over with lattice: for the first forty-eight hours she will endeavor to get out of her confinement, but soon becomes reconciled to it, and then fresh eggs are substituted for the plaster of Paris ones; they will then continue to hatch, without intermission, from three to six months, and even longer; the chickens being withdrawn as soon as hatched, and fresh eggs substituted.* After the third day the eggs are examined, and the clear

---

* The use of turkeys as persistent sitters, or as Mr. Geyelin phrases it "living hatching machines," has been tried with entire success by two amateurs (acquaintances of the author) in the vicinity of Cincinnati.

eggs withdrawn,—which are then sold in the market for new laid; but, as they may be soiled or discolored from having been sat upon, they clean them with water and silver-sand to restore their original whiteness.

The turkeys are taken off their nest once a day to feed and to remove their excrements from the nest; but, after a while, they cease self-feeding, when it is necessary to cram them, and give them some water once a day.

Amongst some places I visited, in company with two of your shareholders, may be mentioned the farm of Madame La Marquise de la Briffe, Chateau de Neuville, Gambais, near Houdan, where we observed twelve turkeys hatching at the same time; here, also, we witnessed the rearing and fattening, which will be alluded to hereafter. In another place, that of Mr. Auché of Gambais, a hatcher by trade, we observed sixty turkeys hatching at the same time; and we were informed that during winter and early spring he had sometimes upwards of one hundred hatching at the same time, and that each turkey continued hatching for at least three months. At the farm of Mr. Louis Mary at St. Julien de Fauçon, near Lizieux in Calvados, I saw a turkey that was then sitting and had been so upwards of six months, and, as I considered it rather cruel, the hatcher, to prove the contrary, took her off the nest and put her in the meadow, and also removed the eggs; the turkey, however, to my surprise, returned immediately to her nest and called in a most plaintive voice for her eggs; then some eggs were placed in a corner of the box, which she instantly drew under her with her beak, and seemed quite delighted. Moreover, I was informed that it was of great economical advantage to employ turkeys to hatch, as they eat very little and get very fat in their state of confinement, and therefore fit for the market any day.

THE REARING OF CHICKENS.

It seems strange that although in all countries the great difficulty of Poultry Breeding is the successful rearing, that no adequate means have ever been devised to counteract the influence of climates. In France, as here, a cold or wet spring is equivalent to a great loss in Poultry, and it seems to be admitted everywhere that cold and wet do not agree with Poultry; therefore, were it not for some novelties I observed in the rearing, to which I shall allude presently, I might well have said that their system is no better than our own; in fact, they show an utter disregard of all sanitary considerations, and without wishing to particularize any establishment, whether public or private, I may state that in even the best conducted, room is left for great improvement in this respect. In some parts of France, where Poultry Breeding is carried on as a trade, they seldom allow a hen to lead the chickens after being hatched, as the hen is more valuable for laying eggs, but they entrust this office either to capons or turkeys, which are said to be far better protectors to the chickens than hens; they require, however, a certain amount of schooling preparatory to being entrusted with their charge, which consists in this: When a turkey has been hatching for some months and shows a disposition to leave off, a glassful of wine is given her in the evening, and a number of chickens are substituted for the eggs; on waking in the morning she kindly takes to them and leads them about, strutting amidst a troop of seventy to one hundred chickens with the dignity of a drum-major. When, however, a troop leader is required that has not been hatching, such as a capon or a turkey, then it is usual to pluck some of their feathers from the breasts, and to give them a glass of wine, and whilst in a state of inebriation to place some chickens under them; on getting sober the next morning they feel that some sudden change has come over them, and as the denuded part is kept warm by the chickens they take also kindly to them.

In conclusion, I feel in justice bound to say that these artificial living protectors are most efficient to shelter chickens in the day-time, and in the evening they are placed with their charge in a shallow box filled with hay, from which they do not move till the door of the room is opened next morning. I must not omit to mention that the chickens are not entrusted to the mother or a leader before they are a week old, and then only in fine weather.

FEEDING AND FATTENING.

THE SYSTEM OF FEEDING Poultry in France is far more judicious than our own; and I may safely assert that I have not noticed a single instance of Poultry being fed on whole grain, as it is the case with us. On inquiring the reason why they fed by meal made into a stiff paste, I was informed that whole grain would be too expensive, produce less eggs, too much fat, and cause more disease when the fowls are fed *ad libitum*, so as to completely fill their crop, which renders the digestion difficult. The food is mostly composed of about one half bran and one half buckwheat, barley, or oat-meal made into a stiff paste, with which the fowls are fed twice a day, namely, at sunrise and sunset; this diet is given indiscriminately to old and young. In some farms, where the Poultry have not the run of meadows, they are provided with a certain amount of animal and vegetable food, which system is so consonant with my own notion, that I will now describe that followed at an establishment already noticed. All the waste of butchers' shops are obtained at the expense of collecting them; these are boiled, the fat skimmed off, which when coagulated is with the waste finely minced and mixed with the meal; after which the waste of the kitchen garden, such as cabbage stalks, are boiled in the liquid and mixed with bran, sour poultry food, etc., which is then given to the pigs, who thrive ad mirably on it. Buckwheat is considered preferable to all other grains as a stimulant to laying eggs, and in winter a certain amount is given whole. The chickens for the first week after being hatched, and in winter for a much longer time, are fed by hand on barley meal mixed with milk, stale bread soaked in water, and green food finely chopped.

FATTENING OF POULTRY.—Whilst the rearing is carried on by farmers, the fattening forms quite a special trade, and chiefly in the hands of cottagers, who purchase the chickens either from farmers or in the market; moreover it is the exclusive trade of a few villages in each Poultry breeding district, such as Goussainville, de Saint Lubin, de La Haye, etc., near Houdan. Villaine and Boce near La Flèche au Mans, also some hamlets near St. Pierre Dive, Lizieux, Calvados. In these localities the system of fattening differs however; the one consists of liquid cramming with barley meal and milk, given by means of a funnel introduced into the throat of the fowl three times a day; this process is exceedingly expeditious, as one person can easily cram at the rate of 60 fowls per hour, and the fattening lasts from fourteen days to three weeks, according to the disposition of the chicken to take fat; the selection of the fattening stock requires some judgment, as some chickens are constitutionally too weak and others have not the frame to receive fat. This system of liquid cramming is principally adopted in the neighborhood of Houdan, and to give an idea of the importance of this trade I will now give a short extract from the pamphlet I was kindly presented with from a most intelligent agriculturalist, Monsieur De la Fosse, Proprietaire à Orval, Goussainville près Houdan :—

"It is to be desired that our excellent and pure breed of Houdan should be propagated in every other country as much as it is in our own, where the Poultry trade has taken such a development that it forms one of the principal sources of riches. A few exact statistics of this trade in our immediate neighborhood will give a correct idea of its importance. At the Markets of Houdan, Dreux, and Nogent le Roi there are sold annually upwards of 6,000,000 head of FAT Poultry, namely :—

	Per Week.	Per month.	Per year.
Houdan	40,000	160,000	1,920,000
Dreux	50,000	200,000	2,400,000
Nogent le Roi	35,000	140,000	1,680,000
Total			6,000,000 "

This does not include the sale of chickens and Poultry which forms a separate trade."

M. De la Fosse also deprecates the use of fat for fattening purposes, as it deteriorates the fineness and flavor of the flesh. In the districts of Le Mans and Normandy the fattening is performed by dry cramming, viz., the meal of barley and buckwheat are made into a stiff paste with milk and water, then formed into pills two inches long and half an inch in diameter; these are dipped into water and forced into the throat of the fowl until the crop is filled, twice a day; it is, however, of importance not to cram a fowl until she has digested the previous meal, as otherwise it might produce inflammation and death.

A most ill-founded notion prevails with all fatteners—that Poultry will fatten much quicker without light or ventilation, and without ever removing their excrements, which makes these places most offensive and unhealthy; no other reason could be assigned to me than that they were quite sure that the smell of the excrements stimulated the fattening; in this there is about as much reason as in the notion our farmers used to entertain that pigs could only thrive in filth. In one place however, which I visited in company with Monsieur Noel, proprietor of the "Lion d'Or" at La Flèche, a most intelligent man, and himself a large farmer, the cottager had provision made for the excrements to fall through the floor of the pen, and on pointing out the innovation he prided himself on his invention, as, said he, I can now remove the manure, and the feathers of the fowls get less dirty, and the birds have also more air. This surely is a step in the right direction.

KILLING AND DRESSING.

This also is a speciality, carried on by men called *Tueurs et Apprêteurs*; they are astonishingly expert in their business, and, unless witnessed as we have done, would appear incredible, that one man can kill and pluck at the rate of one fowl per minute, or sixty per hour: the price paid for this work is about one farthing per head for lean and one halfpenny for fat Poultry. The system of killing differs, however, in this, that whilst in Paris they make a gash in the throat, in the country they stick the Poultry in the back of the roof of the beak, but both cause immediate death; the latter, however, is the cleanest and most desirable. They deprecate our system of twisting the neck as cruel, discoloring the flesh, and causing early putrefaction of the coagulated blood. When a man plucks he has three baskets near him, into which he drops the feathers according to size; and the reason of plucking the fowls instantaneously after death is the great saving in time, and the prevention of tearing the skin, which cannot well be avoided when the fowl once gets cold.

The lean fowls are immediately emptied of their intestines, but not so with the fat stock, which contain a large quantity of valuable fat, which is used for basting, and to give flavor to lean Poultry.

With chickens they take care to leave the down on, as an index of their age, and in all fowls they leave about half-a-dozen feathers in the rump, which gives a very pretty appearance.

As soon as the fowl is plucked, and before cold, it is laid on its back on a bench, and wrapped round with a wet linen cloth to mould its shape, and to give the skin a finer appearance; however, they use no flour, as with us, to give an old hen the appearance of a chicken.

The fat Poultry is drawn and dressed **by cooks**; they make an incision under the **leg to withdraw** the intestines, **by** which means the fowl is **not disfigured.**

UTILIZING THE WASTE PRODUCTS.

Poultry Manure.—In France, as well as **in our** own country, most **eminent** chemists have proved by analysis that Poultry manure is a most valuable fertilizer, and yet for want of a proper system in housing Poultry it has as yet not been rendered available to rural economy. In France, as in England, the Poultry manure is left to accumulate in the Poultry homes, to the loss of farmers and to the detriment **of** the health of fowls.

The Feathers are carefully collected and sorted, **and when well** dried sold to dealers.

The Intestines are boiled, the fat skimmed **off**, which is sold separate; the intestines are then minced as food for Poultry, and the liquid is used for feeding pigs.

The Combs and Kidneys **are sold to pastry cooks**—the first for decorating and the latter for flavoring **pies.**

The *Head*, *Neck*, *and Feet* are sold to hotels, restaurants, **etc.,** for flavoring sauces, **or boiled down to make chicken jelly.**

THE SYSTEM OF SELLING

Poultry in France is far preferable to our own, although, in my opinion, it would be still better were Poultry **sold** by weight. However, a farmer or merchant who consigns Poultry to Paris is sure to obtain a true return of whatever they fetched, as he does not rely, as with **us**, on the honesty of a dealer.

At the wholesale Poultry market, **La Vallée,** in Paris, where all Poultry, dead or alive, is forwarded from all parts of France, there are a number of licensed agents **to** whom the Poultry is consigned, and **who sell it by auction to the highest** bidder; this market is a curious scene, **and worth seeing, from four till nine in** the morning, where **thousands of crates of all descriptions of Poultry are** disposed **of, and** cleared out, before twelve o'clock in the day.

Every village has **its weekly markets, where farmers and** their **wives** bring their produce for sale, **in preference to** selling it at the farmyard. The police regulations **in these markets are** strictly enforced. **The** various products are **classified before the** market begins. Each **person** is bound to keep **his assigned place, and** not allowed even to uncover his goods, **and much less to sell, before the** bell rings, under a fine of **five francs. At the ringing of the bell,** the bustle to uncover, the rush **of buyers, and the chattering, is worth while to witness. The dealers** and merchants take up their stand outside the market, where they send all the products they purchase. The seller has a ticket given him, with the purchase price on it, and is paid on delivery of the goods at the dealer's stand. It seems almost incredible to believe that even in some village markets, within two hours, such a vast amount of business can be transacted with the greatest order and decorum. Some merchants will purchase from 2000 to 3000 pounds of butter; others, 20,000 to 30,000 eggs, or some thousand head of Poultry, etc.; all which are taken to their warehouse to be sorted, packed, and perhaps forwarded the same day either to London or Paris. I may add that the current price for every commodity is fixed and known immediately after the market opens, and depends entirely on the demand and supply. For instance, fat chickens fetched four shillings each; twelve eggs, seven pence; butter, ten pence per pound, etc.

For the foregoing information, I am mainly indebted to Mr. H. Lindon, jun., a most obliging gentleman, who represents at Lizieux the Messrs. Lindon Brothers & Co. of London, general merchants; in his company I have visited several farms, and attended market, at which he makes purchases of butter, grain, etc., for the London market.

BREEDS, ETC.

There are three perfectly distinct breeds, all very characteristic in their appearance; and, when pure, they are very true to all their points. [The author proceeds to give descriptions of the three breeds noticed in the body of this book, and of these only, which we omit.]

HOUDAN FOWL.

It must be admitted, that most of the farmers near Houdan know as little of the pure Houdan breed as those of La Flèche and Crèvecœur know of theirs; and, if you were to order some first class birds of them, irrespective of price, they would with good conscience forward fowls of a large size—but, from a want of knowledge, some cross breeds. To illustrate this, I may mention that I could have purchased, at the markets in those respective localities, splendid thorough-bred specimens for about three shillings, the price of common fowls,—but which were worth in France even one pound each. There are, however, in each locality, some persons who take an interest in their pure breeds, particularly since they have been encouraged by the reward of prizes from Poultry exhibitions.

CAPONAGE.

There seems to exist a considerable difference of opinion in various parts of France as to the necessity of castrating young cocks for fattening purposes. In some localities they pretend that when cocks are not allowed to associate with the opposite sex that they will attain, when fattened, a greater weight, and be much finer as regards flavor of flesh; others again say that when a cock is castrated, it can be kept till a more mature age without deteriorating its quality, and by this, attain an extraordinary weight when fattened, besides making them useful as troop leaders of chickens, as before described. I cannot decide which of the two systems is the best or most advantageous, more than I can decide about the two systems of cramming, without making experiments; this much, however, I have noticed, that virgin cocks fatten very readily, and fetch prices as high as capons.

TECHNICAL TERMS. 117

TERMS AND TECHNICALITIES.

The Terms explained by reference to the above engraving, are as follows:

A—The Face.
B—The Comb.
C—The Wattles.
D—The Ear.
E—The Ear-lobe.
F—Neck-hackle.
G—Saddle feathers or Back-hackle.
H—Breast, extending to the thighs.
J—Upper wing-coverts.
K—Lower wing-coverts.
L—Flight feathers.
M—The Tail.
N—Sickle Tail-feathers.
O—Tail Coverts.
P—The Thighs.
R—The Legs.

Some other terms are the following:

Broody—Inclined to sit or incubate.
Carunculated.—Covered with fleshy protuberances like a Turkey-cock's head and neck, or the head of a Musk drake.
Casque.—The helmet-like, fleshy protuberance or comb of the Guinea Fowl

Clutch.—A number of eggs sat upon by a fowl, or the number of chickens brought off.

Clung.—Shrunk and stringy, applied to flesh which has never been properly fattened, or which has fallen away after being fat.

Crest.—The Tuft of Feathers which some fowls, like the Polands, have upon their heads.

Deaf Ear.—A name improperly applied to the true ear of the fowl.—A shallow hole, or depression with a hair-like covering.

Dubbing.—Trimming off the combs and wattles of Game fowls, for fighting, or for exhibition.

Dunghills.—Common Fowls; those of mixed breeds, not crossed with definite purpose, or those of a breed degenerated.

Fluff.—Soft downy feathers in masses upon certain parts of fowls—as upon the rumps and thighs of Cochins.

Moulting.—Periodical shedding and renewal of feathers.

Pea-comb.—A tripple comb—a principal comb with a small one on each side.

Poult.—A young turkey, or other gallinaceous fowl, before it takes on the full plumage of a mature bird.

Rose-comb.—A full, broad, flat comb, called also "Double comb."

Top Knot.—See Crest.

Vulture Hocked.—Having the feathers upon the thigh project backward below and beyond the "hock" joints.

INDEX.

Basket for Transporting and Showing Fowls 105
Breeding from Young Fowls desirable.................... 19
Breeding—Necessity of Fresh Blood 20
BREEDS:
   Bantams, Golden and Silver Seabrights, Description. etc.—Characteristics not well fixed—Weight—Black Bantams—Feather-legged, etc.—Layers, Sitters, and Nurses.... 70
   Bolton Greys 66
   Brahma Pootras—Origin—First Appearance—Description—Opinions of Poultry Fanciers—Estimation of Brahma's in Different Countries—High Prices—Sitters and Nurses—Layers and Market Fowls... ,34-41
   Cochin China Fowls—Introduction and Dissemination—Description—Colors—Changes of Plumage with Age—Early Layers and Sitters.62-66
   Creole Fowls.. 66
   Crevecœur Fowls...................................... 77
   Dominiques.. 66
   Dorkings—Antiquity—First brought to the U. S.—Varieties—Value as Layers, Market Birds, etc.,—May not be bred in-and-in—Estimation in England—Grey preferred to White variety............... 41-48
   French Breeds, with Description of each............... 75-80
   French Methods of Rearing, Fattening, etc. (Appendix)...... 107-116
   Games—Antiquity of Cock-fighting—Characteristics and Description—Dubbing—Cutting-out—Fitness for the Table—Lord Derby's breed—Good Sitters and Nurses 54-59
   Game Fowls fed so as to harden Plumage 105
   Hamburgs, Golden and Silver-penciled—Origin and Description—Non-sitters—Guards 66-67
   Houdan Fowls 77-115
   La Fleche Fowls..................................... 79
   Leghorn Fowls—Source, Characteristics, Pure type, etc... 73
   Malays—Origin and Description—Chickens—Colors—Hardiness—Pugnacity 60-62
   Poland Fowls—Black, and Spangled—Description—Mal-formation common... 68-70
   Spanish Fowls—Description—Color—Form—Large Eggs—Difficult to rear—White Feathers in Chickens—Constant Layers.......... 49-53
   Spanish Fowls confined before Exhibiting............. 105
Chickens—Care of Young................................ 20-21
Coop for Fattening Fowls............................... 22-25
Coop for Hen and Chickens.............................. 20
Coop for very Early Chickens........................... 103
Cramming Fowls.. 25-26
Degeneracy of Blood, How shown........................ 32
DISEASES:
   Arising from filthy Water 22
   Bumble-footed 11
   Crop-bound... 26
   Dropsy caused by stimulating food.................... 18
   Gapes.. 30
   Indigestion 25-31
   Over-feeding.. 18
   Roup... 29
   Scouring... 31
   Weak Knees.. 11-32
DUCKS:
   Aylesbury 95
   Aylesbury, Opinions of popular Writers and Poultry Fanciers....... 96-97
   Enemies of... 95
   Feeding and Management............................... 93
   Musk or Muscovy...................................... 97
   Musk—Various Authorities on......................... 97-98
   Rouen—Characteristics of, etc........................ 100
Ducklings in the down die of wet........................ 94

INDEX.

Fattening Food and Time of Feeding, 23—See also Appendix. 112
FATTENING FOWLS, 22—See also Appendix 111
    Age most suitable for...... 27
    Cause of tough flesh in.. 27-28
    Killed after Fasting 28
    Shelter essential to.. 27
    Time required for......................................24-26
Feeding Fowls, 15-16-24—Also Appendix...........................111
Feeding after Traveling or Fasting................................ 16
FOOD :
    Amount consumed by Fowls 15
    For Show birds...105
    For Young Chickens.. 21
    Grass, essential 15-24
    Insects, etc., as food 17
    Raw meat unsuitable... 16
    Stimulating food, Effect of................................... 18
    To make Hens lay.. 18
    Vegetable food for Fowls 15
FOWLS :
    Avoid draughts.. 11
    Mentioned in Scriptures and in the Classics.................... 9
    Origin of Domestic.... 3
GEESE :
    Breeding Geese.. 90
    Disease of, from short feed................................... 90
    Habits at pasture... 90
    African 92
    Bremen 92
    China... 92
    Domestic 89
    Embden... 92
    Guinea.. 92
    Toulouse.. 92
Goose-house... 90
Goose Pasture... 90
Goose—Varieties of the.. 92
Goslings—Food for... 91
Goslings—Young, killed by hot Sun................................. 91
Guinea Fowl—Habits—Eggs—Hide their Nests—How to find them—Mate in
    Pairs—Breeding, etc......................................86-88
Hatching in the natural way....................................... 20
Hatching by Artificial means—Forced, by Turkeys, etc. (Appendix)......108-109
Killing and Dressing as done systematically in France.............113
Laying and Sitting Hens, Kept apart............................... 13
Lice.. 31
Nest Boxes 12
Nests—Grass Sods for Bottoms of................................... 13
Perches for Roosts.. 11
Poultry for Exhibitions—Breeding and Management of..........102-106
Poultry for Exhibitions—Fighting or Cowed fowls to be avoided in...........104
POULTRY HOUSES :
    Plan of Cheap.. 14
    Divisions of.. 12
    Earth floors for..12-14
    Fowls only in.. 12
    Should be lofty.. 10
    Ventilation of..11-14
    Why desirable.. 10
Poultry Yard—Covered run.. 13
Turkies—Colors—Hardiness—Habits—Breeding—Choice of Breeding Birds—
    Cock destroys Eggs—Hen a faithful Sitter—Care of chickens......81-86
Water—Purity and Freshness essential 21
Washing Poultry ... .105
White Fowls to have Freedom before Exhibiting them.................105

www.ingramcontent.com/pod-product-compliance
Lightning Source LLC
Chambersburg PA
CBHW031619170426
43195CB00037B/1185